Attired

Perspectives on Historical Costume

Edited by
Dr Damayanthie Eluwawalage
Delaware State University

Series on the History of Art

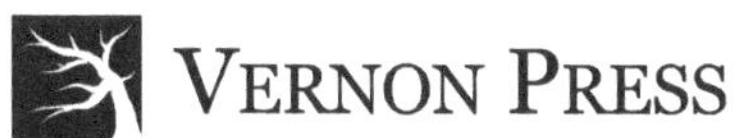

www.vernonpress.com

In the Americas:
Vernon Press
1000 N West Street, Suite 1200
Wilmington, Delaware, 19801
United States

In the rest of the world:
Vernon Press
C/Sancti Espiritu 17,
Malaga, 29006
Spain

Series on the History of Art

Library of Congress Control Number: 2024930736

ISBN: 979-8-8819-0190-5

Also available: 978-1-64889-852-5 [Hardback]; 979-8-8819-0001-4 [PDF, E-Book]

Cover design by Vernon Press.

Table of Contents

List of Figures

Introduction

This publication explores the integrative narratives of historical costume in the novel ecumenical perspective of literature, leisure, ornamentation, customs/traditions, and theoretical contexts. The adaptation, mutation, and transformation of attire are the result of complex interactions between many factors such as economic conditions, political conditions, social conditions, psychological conditions, and technology. The meanings encoded in the costume are one of the noticeable hallmarks of any society. This proposed book investigates multidisciplinary topics; for instance, "From Pattern to Pate: An Examination of Early Modern Embroidered English Head-Coverings and their Sources," examines embellishments such as needlework and embroidery, which was regarded as a pervasive practice during the early modern era in England (and elsewhere). This skill was used to decorate a vast number of items of clothing and furnishings in all socio-economic levels, including the ubiquitous head coverings: the cap for men and the coif for women. These items were, at their most basic, constructed from rough homespun linen to the finest and sheerest batiste, and could be very plain or intricately decorated with silk, gold, lace, spangles, and pulled and drawn whitework. At the most extreme end, they were blatant status symbols of wealth and power, just as a Hermes scarf would be today. The patterns for these designs were an important part of the chain of production. In fact, a key source for many patterns included the manuscripts written by Thomas Trevelyon in the early seventeenth century. He was a draughtsman who created a number of patterns for decorative arts, including patterns specific to embroidery and, especially, embroidered caps. The study will examine these patterns, show how they were utilized in needlework, and discuss the importance of caps and coifs as an item of clothing at this time. In relation to sports and related-costumes, "It to Win It: The Evolution of Fightwear in Mixed Martial Arts Combat Sports," focuses on the historical concept of fight, physical encounter, combat, or bout and its connection with related-attire. As the study explains, sanctioned, licensed mixed martial arts (MMA) combat sports are some of the most popular events taking place around the world today, with some organizations boasting their fight cards are available to view in over on hundred and fifty countries and which can be seen by up to 2.7 billion people, live, as the action happens. Although everyone in every location where the event is being telecast may not be watching the contest, it is true that MMA has gone from a relatively unknown, untelevised, unsanctioned sport thirty years ago to a global phenomenon today. Similar to all sports, MMA has changed significantly since its inception as it has grown in popularity, specifically with regard to the fightwear, or costumes, that are worn by mixed martial artists, especially those worn by fighters in the Ultimate Fighting Championship promotion since its formation in 1993. It was in the first UFC fight card where combatants could wear anything they wanted, such as full keikogi, lycra, or spandex wrestling singlets or even wrestling briefs seen in the World Wrestling Federation, now known as World Wrestling Entertainment, Inc. The choice of fightwear by the fighter could dramatically alter the way combatants engaged with each other. Today, fightwear is regulated by the promotion and the sanctioning body, whether it be an individual state commission or a nation's regulating body. In the case of the Ultimate Fighting Championship, both the promotion and the sanctioning body, which is the national Association of Boxing Commissions, regulate fightwear from the clothing the fighters put on to the gloves they wear, and their groin protection as well as their gum shields are also regulated. The evolution of fight costumes is interesting as it not only demonstrates the utility of the attire but also the changing rules due to a variety of influences external to the fighter's preference, not the least of which are the demands of the fight promotors of the MMA organization, the governing commission and the fans; In the context of clothing and literature, "Attire in Virgil's Aeneid," analyses the contribution of dress to the narrative process of Virgil's Aeneid, which in the West possesses a readership second only to the Bible. The epic commemorates Rome, destined to rule the world, when Octavian became the first emperor as Augustus Caesar. Hailed as canonical while still being written and celebrated by Emperor Augustus in 17 BCE as a masterpiece of poetry and patriotism, the Aeneid was swiftly adopted as both "school text and part of the furniture of the mind for educated Romans."[1] Seen as the external trappings of an internal quest, as allegorical poetry where the concrete stands in for ideas, the Aeneid inspires both sight and insight in large part by its use of material culture, often in the form of items of dress. Consequently, this chapter examines select narratives constructed around vestments, and discusses how Virgil directs micro-level, personal clothing items to probe and question macrolevel themes such as the cost of war and empire-building. Using modern western social theory, it tracks dress as it carries and transmits culturally ascribed messages

---

[1] Charles Martindale, *Introduction: The Classic of all Europe,* in "The Cambridge Companion to Virgil" ed. Charles Martindale (Cambridge, U.K: Cambridge UP, 1997), 1s.

that expand metaphysical and historical meaning in this early cannon of literature where clothing items act as devices to shape and construct the narrative, mold character, and advance the plot. This study considers how clothing images embedded within this ancient volume function to convey the cultural convictions of the civilizations from which the text arises. As "Historical Costume: Acknowledging the Distinctiveness Between the Centuries and Epochs" examines, in any historical study, literary texts should be interpreted within the appropriate historical context, especially when analyzing costumes. For example, in *Daily Life in Ancient Rome,*[2] Jerome Carcopino states, "If Roman life is not to become lost in anachronisms or petrified in abstraction, we must study it within a strictly defined period." The differences between centuries are significantly varied in the context of human deportment, customs, traditions, and attitudes.[3] In fact, the pursuit of etiquette has been a societal concern for centuries.[4] Manners and deportment are constantly transformed with changing society; therefore, these social behaviors should not be regarded merely as details of little consequence; they are an expression of a particular era as much as any other outward manifestation. Thus, according to Roland Barthes, "When we examine how clothes define an individual, we must also set the man or woman within the context of their place and time," as the differences in clothing styles between the centuries are significant.[5] Cutting and construction techniques also varied considerably from century to century as each era produced its own unique decorations and silhouettes.[6] Clothes represent an art form ascending out of a particular period and environment. According to Francois Boucher, costume and its application and meaning have varied with each period.[7] Differences in fashion theories also reflect different eras, and the chapter will explore those pertinent fashion theories between the fifteenth and nineteenth centuries. For example, nineteenth-century theorists, such as Thorstein Veblen and Georg Simmel,

---

[2] Jerome Carcopino, *Daily Life in Ancient Rome* (London: Penguin Books, 1941), 9.

[3] Joan Wildeblood, *The Polite World: A Guide to English Manners and Deportment* (London: Davis Poynter Ltd, 1965).

[4] Joseph Dent, *Australian Etiquette: Rules and Usage of the Best Society* (London: D. E. McConnell, 1980).

[5] Anne Hollander, *Sex and Suits* (New York: Alfred A. Knoff, 1995).

[6] Gordon Willis & David Midgley, *Fashion Marketing: An Anthology of View Points and Perspectives* (London: Allen and Unwin Ltd, 1973), 12.

[7] Francois Boucher, A History of Costume in the West (London: Thames and Hudson, 1966), 5-6.

regarded differentiation and stratification as essential pre-conditions of fashion. Twentyth-century theorist Herbert Blumer, on the other hand, regards fashion as an expression of collective behavior; that is, the fashion mechanism appears not in response to a need for class differentiation and class emulation but in response to a wish to be in fashion. Also, the psychological, sociological, and gender aspects of costume will be discussed in theoretical contexts.

Bibliography

Boucher, Francois. *A History of Costume in the West.* London: Thames and Hudson, 1966.

Carcopino, Jerome. *Daily Life in Ancient Rome.* London: Penguin Books, 1941.

Dent, Joseph. *Australian Etiquette: Rules and Usage of the Best Society.* London: D. E. McConnell, 1980.

Hollander, Anne. *Sex and Suits,* New York: Alfred A. Knoff, 1995.

Martindale, Charles. *Introduction: The Classic of all Europe,* in "The Cambridge Companion to Virgil" ed. Charles Martindale. Cambridge, U.K: Cambridge UP, 1997.

Wildblood, Joan. *The Polite World: A Guide to English Manners and Deportment.* London: Davis Poynter Ltd, 1965.

Willis, Gordon. & Midgley, David. *Fashion Marketing: An Anthology of View Points and Perspectives.* London: Allen and Unwin Ltd, 1973.

Chapter 1

Pattern to Pate: An Examination of Early Modern Embroidered English Head-Coverings and their Sources

Christy Gordon Baty and Erin Harvey Moody

Harvard University

Abstract: Embellishments such as needlework and embroidery were regarded as a pervasive practice during the early modern era in England (and elsewhere). This skill was used to decorate a vast number of items of clothing and furnishings in all socio-economic levels. These items were constructed from rough homespun linen to the finest and sheerest batiste, and could be very plain or intricately decorated with silk, gold, lace, spangles, and pulled and drawn whitework. Also, they were blatant status symbols of wealth and power. The patterns for these designs were an important part of the chain of production. The study will examine these patterns, show how they were utilized in needlework, and discuss the importance of caps and coifs as an item of clothing at this time.

Keywords: Head-coverings, Embroidery, Needlework, Early-modern England, Coif, Caps, Status symbols, Spangles, Whitework, Trevelyon patterns

***

Women's coif and men's cap were typical of the ubiquitous head coverings in the sixteenth and seventeenth-centuries in England. Though more often made of plain linen and intended only as functional head coverings, caps and coifs that were highly embellished with needlework marked them out as exceptional, a proclamation of wealth and an assertion of status. Popular in England during this time period, embroidered caps and coifs occupied a liminal space between the private and public, similar to a home's stratified areas of relative accessibility to increasing exclusivity. Intended only to be worn in the intimacy of one's own home, they were expensive objects of personal display that were meant to impress visitors. While there are only a few depictions of men and women wearing their embroidered caps and coifs (Figure 1.1), there are a significant number of these objects extant in collections today (Figure 1.2 and Figure 1.3).

Figure 1.1: A Lady and Her Two Children

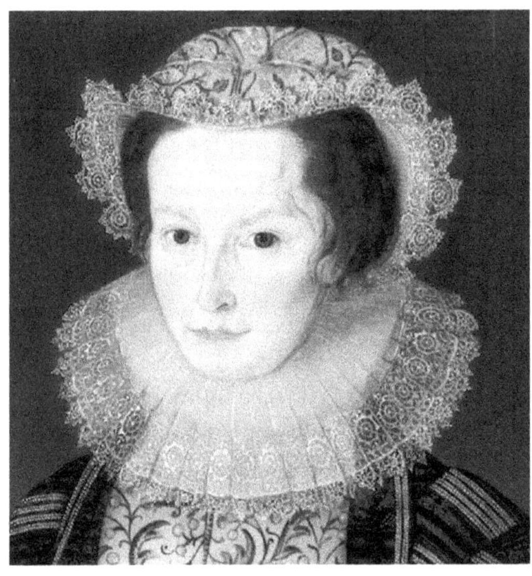

https://commons.wikimedia.org/w/index.php?title=File:A_Lady_and_Her_Two_Children_-_Google_Art_Project.jpg&oldid=722137325 (accessed January 24, 2023).

Figure 1.2: Woman's Coif, 1600-1625

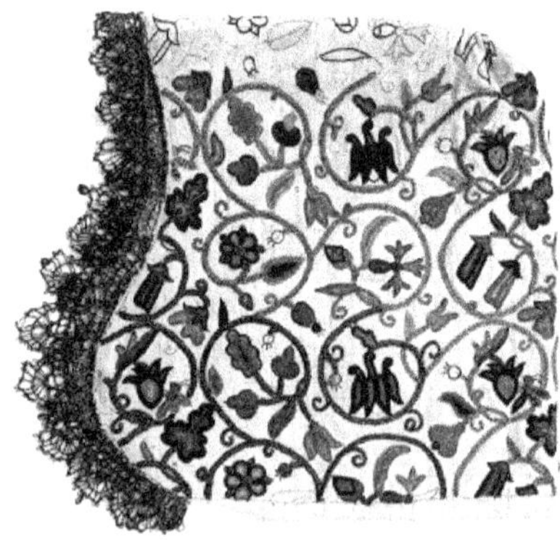

Artist Unknown. Victoria and Albert Museum, London. Photo permission by Relics in Situ.

Figure 1.3: Man's Cap, 1600-1629.

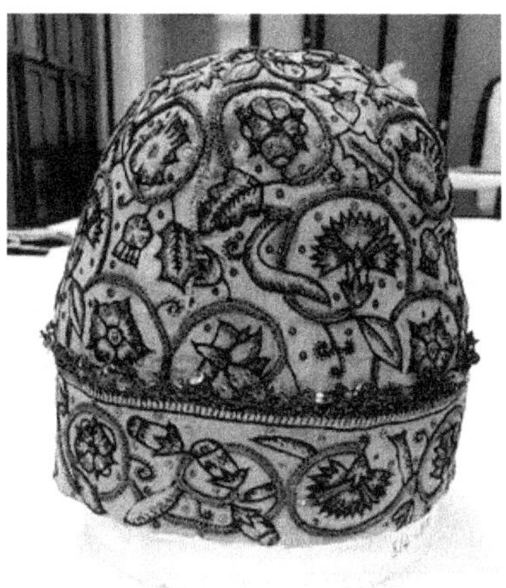

Artist Unknown. Victoria and Albert Museum, London. Photo permission by Relics in Situ.

Examining the materiality of these objects and the context in which they were worn can provide insight into the value of needlework, the patterns and sources that inspired them, and the lives of the people who owned, created, and even preserved them.

A woman's coif and a man's cap were basic, fundamental close-fitting head coverings in early modern England, as is evidenced by paintings, illuminations, and drawings from this time period. Usually made of linen, or, in specialized circumstances, silk, these head coverings fulfilled several functions including to cover a person's hair to keep it clean. Women tended to cover their hair with their coif as a sign of their married status.[1] Both men and women wore their caps and coifs to keep their heads warm, whether inside by themselves or outside under a hat. Noticeably, the shape of these head coverings was quite consistent.

Besides the coif and cap, head coverings encompassed a wide range of items, including hats, hoods, cauls, and veils. While a hat is a hat at its most basic level, the variations in head coverings by class level and gender and the supplies used to make and embellish these objects introduced a broad spectrum of material goods. These variations asserted a curated image of a person's place in society, which was a purpose that all clothes were intended to communicate. Early

[1] Ninya Mikhaila and Jane Malcolm-Davies, *The Tudor Tailor: Reconstructing Sixteenth Century Dress,* (Hollywood: Costume and Fashion Press, 2006), 28-30.

modern English culture was extremely hierarchical, and displays of clothing (as well as other material objects such as homes and furnishings, books, etc) were a necessary and important way to assert status, to let other people know what rank you were, and how you expected to be treated.[2]

While people of all classes almost always wore a head covering of some sort, indoors and out, the scope of this article will focus on the creation, wear, context, and significance of embroidered caps and coifs. This necessarily limits the socio-economic classes we will be discussing to primarily wealthy merchants and middling sort, the gentry, and the nobility. These are the people who would be able to afford the expense of creating or purchasing the materials, time, and the skilled expertise the creation of these head coverings required.

Figure 1.4: Lady Wearing Embroidered Waistcoat

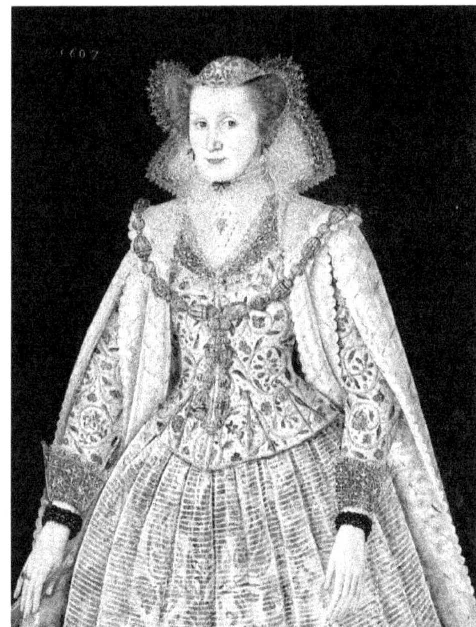

https://commons.wikimedia.org/wiki/File:Circle_of_Robert_Peake_Portrait_of_a_lady,_wearing_an_embroidered_waistcoat.jpg (accessed January 10, 2023).

---

[2] Thomas Tolley, "Visual Culture" in *Gentry culture in late-medieval England,* ed. By Raduca Radelescu and Alison Truelove (Manchester: Manchester UP, 2005), 167-182; Ruth Goodman, *How to Be a Tudor a Dawn-to-Dusk Guide to Tudor Life,* (New York: Liveright Publishing Corporation, a division of W.W. Norton & Company, 2017), 55.

There is pictorial evidence that women of all classes wore some form of coif. Lower down the social structure, these were made from plain linen, though even laborers could add embellishments, including whitework edgings as well as some bone lace, modernly called bobbin lace. Indeed, these types of embellishments would serve not only as decoration but, more importantly, reinforce the edges of the linen cap and extend the wear of the object by preventing fraying and unraveling. It is only higher up the social scale that there is evidence of both plain and embroidered coifs for women and embroidered caps for men that included metal thread embroidery (silver and silver-gilt), polychrome silks, and additional decorative materials like silver gilt spangles and silver gilt bobbin lace (Figure 1.4).

It is important to keep in mind that those higher up the social scale did not mean only the elite. There is a concept in popular culture that decorative embroidery was so expensive that it was out of reach of all but the most affluent members of society. That may be true in some instances, including larger garments like a fully embellished woman's jacket or a man's doublet. The very fact that caps and coifs were smaller in scale made them more accessible. For instance, the records of the Wardens of Orphans in Sandwich detail the upbringing of Thomasina Wolters from 1588 through 1594. She was left a small but decent income from a house producing a rental of over ten pounds a year. Thomasina's expenses detail the cost of her boarding and education with Mrs. Smythe, including an item "to buy her some silke to Worke her a koyf & other such like."[3] Based on this information, Thomasina was definitely a girl of the middling sort and was able to, and even expected to, learn decorative needlework and make and wear her own embellished coif.

Styles of head coverings were highly situational. There are images of women wearing plain, unembellished coifs outside, often with hats on top of the coif, but there is only pictorial evidence of embroidered caps and coifs being worn in indoor settings, as is depicted in A Village Festival attributed to Marcus Gheeraerts the Elder, c. 1575. The same rule applies to men who are depicted with embroidered caps in indoor settings, and there are no images of men with similar caps outside. The implication is that these embellished, expensive items of clothing would not be exposed to the weather or the general conditions of everyday life in Elizabethan England. These were strictly for at-home displays of wealth and status.

---

[3] Thomas Dorman, "The Sandwich Book of Orphans," *Archaeologia Cantiana* 16 (1886): 189.

The Making of Caps and Coifs

Given the elaborate materials and skills needed to create these needlework embellishments, why were these particular items embroidered? This was a time period when needlework became increasingly popular, and extended from clothing and worn accessories to chairs, hangings, cushions, and other home furnishings to objects like mirrors and small caskets. Embroidery on all of these objects asserted a certain social status, and each object that could be decorated with needlework was another opportunity for display. Additionally, embroidered coifs and caps were relatively small and finite endeavors that required less time and fewer materials and, therefore, less expense than an entire jacket or skirt, both of which were still also popular embroidered clothing items. This applies to both professionally and domestically produced caps and coifs.

There are a number of needlework specific pattern books that were printed and reprinted on the continent, with each printer improving on previous versions, adding more material, and borrowing heavily from other versions.[4] These pattern books were imported into England and their designs show up in a variety of extant objects. There were also several extremely popular English needlework pattern books, including the *Scholehouse for the Needle* and *The Needle's Excellency.*[5] The wide availability of these pattern books particularly benefitted domestic needleworkers who did not always have access to professional draughtsmen, as an embroidery studio would.

Other types of books, such as herbals, emblem books, natural history books, and even illustrated frontispieces in devotional books like the Bible or the Psalms, were rich sources for individual elements like flowers and animals, as well as entire scenes (Figure 1.5). Individual sheets of images and other ephemera were also a source of patterns. Consequently, similar images recur frequently. For instance, squirrels appear in a number of illustrations of natural history books in the same posture: crouching, holding a nut to the mouth, with a fluffy tail held high. The vast majority of squirrels illustrated at this time are represented in this pose, and squirrels in English embroidery follow this same pose (Figure 1.6 and Figure 1.7).

---

[4] Femke Speelberg, "Fashion & Virtue: Textile Patterns and the Print Revolution, 1520–1620" in The Metropolitan Museum of Art Bulletin, v. 73, No. 2 (Fall, 2015) (Metropolitan Museum of Art, 2015), 21.

[5] Richard Shorleyker. *A Schole-house, for the Needle,* United Kingdom: [Pinted [sic] in Shoe-lane, at the signe of the Faulcon, by Richard Shorleyker.], 1632.

Figure 1.5: Emblems for Needlework

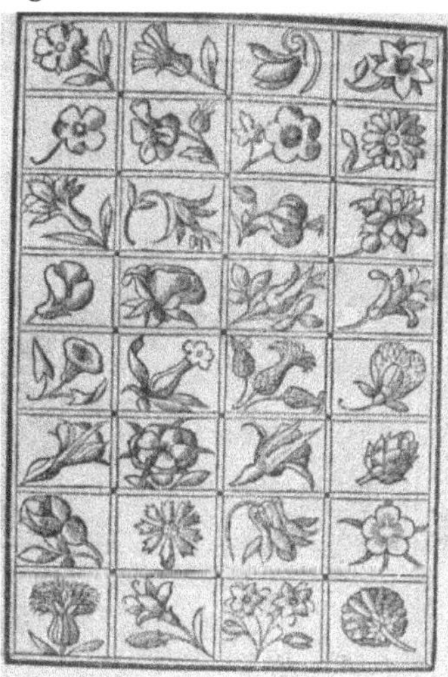

https://archive.org/details/tagliente1530operabnfbtv1b10548051/page/n27/mode/2up. (accessed December 14, 2022).

Figure 1.6: Engraving of a Squirrel by Peter Stent

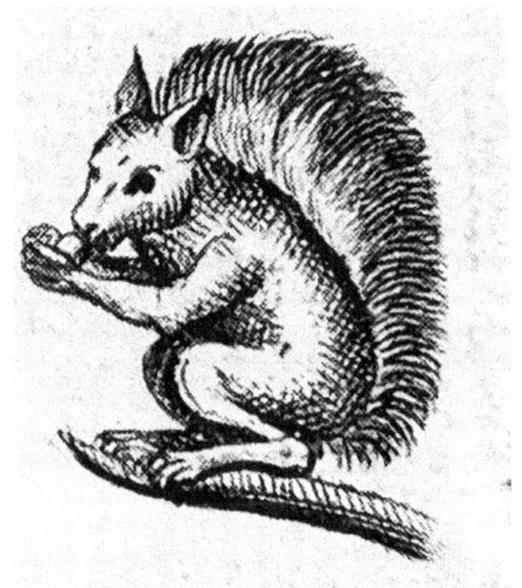

A Book of flowers, fruits, beasts, birds, and flies: Seventeenth-century patterns for embroiderers, printed and sold by Peter Stent, 1662.[6] https://archive.org/details/bookofflowersfru0000unse/page/n3/mode/2up (accessed September 10, 2023).

[6] Peter Stent. *A Book of flowers, fruits, beasts, birds, and flies: seventeenth-century patterns for embroiderers printed and sold by Peter Stent.* Austin: Curious Works Press, 1995.

Figure 1.7: Woman's Coif detail, 1600-1625.

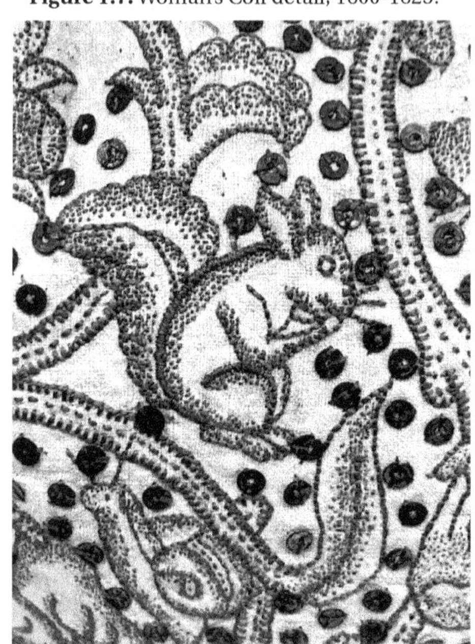

Artist Unknown. Victoria and Albert Museum, London. Photo permission by Relics in Situ.

Figure 1.8: Two coiling stem or rinceau motifs from Modelbuch Nehwens, Stickens, and Wirckens, Christian Egenolff.

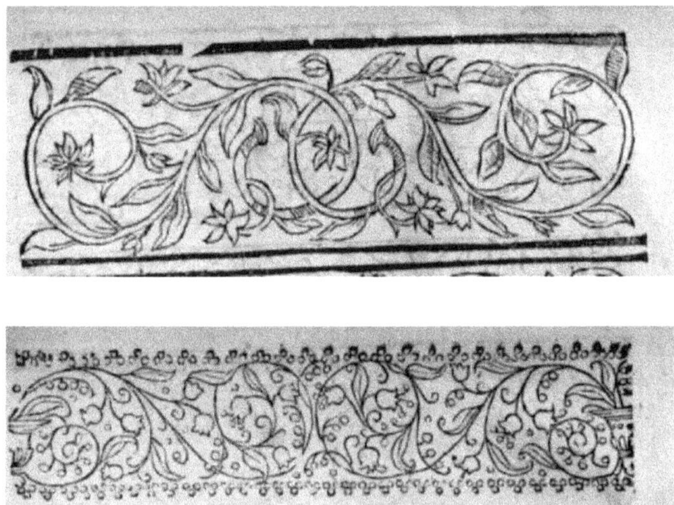

https://archive.org/details/egenloff155modelbuchbsb/page/n15/mode/2up (accessed September 10, 2023).

The influence of gardens on Elizabethan embroidery designs and patterns cannot be overstated. Images of fruits, flowers, fauna, and insects were often combined with the coiling stem layout, which was the most popular composition on caps and coifs: the coiling stem is a stylized curvilinear vine with alternating scrolls from which foliage, flowers, and fruits grow.[7] Coiling stems can be made with all one leaf in a repeating pattern or with a mixture of unrelated flora. This motif is closely related to the rinceau motif, the continental renaissance style of coiling branches with foliage popular in architectural and decorative arts embellishments. Below are several examples of the coiling stem design. The first are two coiling stem patterns from a German pattern book printed in 1555 (Figure 1.8), and the other is a coiling stem worked in silk and metal thread on a man's cap from the Cleveland Museum of Art (Figure 1.9).

Figure 1.9: Elizabethan Man's Cap

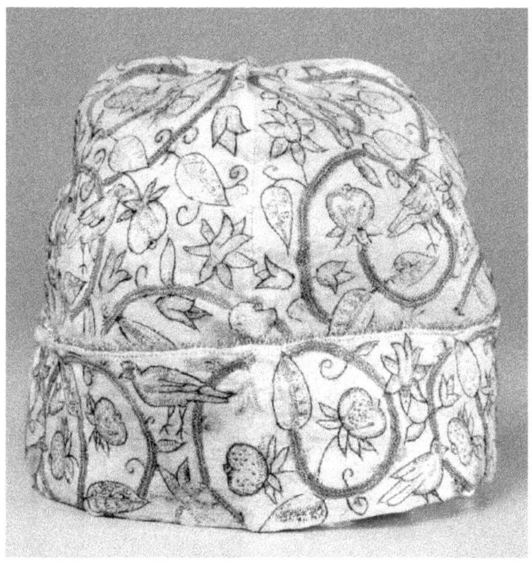

https://commons.wikimedia.org/wiki/File:England,_Elizabethan_Period,_late_16th_century_-_Man%27s_Cap_-_1942.165_-_Cleveland_Museum_of_Art.tif (accessed December 16, 2022).

[7] Susan North, "An Instrument of profit, pleasure and of ornament": Embroidered Tudor and Jacobean Dress Accessories," in *English embroidery from the Metropolitan Museum of Art, 1580-1700: 'twixt art and nature*, ed. Andrew Morrall and Melinda Watt (New Have and London: Yale UP, 2006), 39-56.

A red silk embroidered woman's coif in the Victoria and Albert Museum exemplifies this common coiling stem motif (Figure 1.10).[8] The needlework design combines grape leaves, roses, pansies, pears, and foxgloves on the same vine. As was usual for all examples of Elizabethan and Jacobean embroidery, birds, insects, and animals are often added without regard to scale. This cap includes squirrels, robins, butterflies, snails, and caterpillars executed in approximately the same size as each other. The goal of this type of needlework was not accuracy or realism. Rather, it was to create a sense of abundance. The Ashmolean Museum collection includes a man's cap, which also utilizes the garden motif with details of cornflowers, borage, honeysuckle, strawberries, and foxgloves, all botanically unrelated.[9]

Figure 1.10: Woman's Coif, 1600-1625

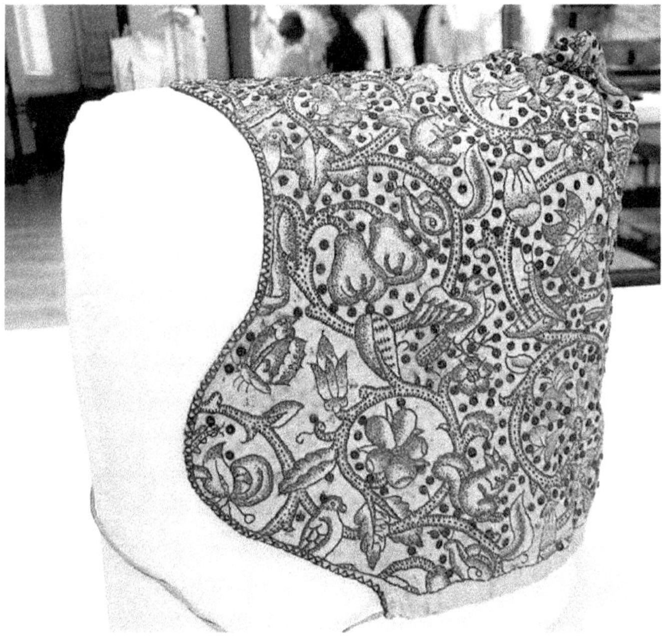

Artist Unknown. Victoria and Albert Museum, London. Photo permission by Relics in Situ.

---

[8] Unknown. Coif. 1600-1625, linen and silk thread, Victoria and Albert Museum, London. accession number T.32-1936.

[9] Unknown. Coif. Early 17th Century, linen and silk thread, Ashmolean Museum, Oxford. accession number WA2014.71.52.

Figure 1.11: Woman's Coif. 17th century

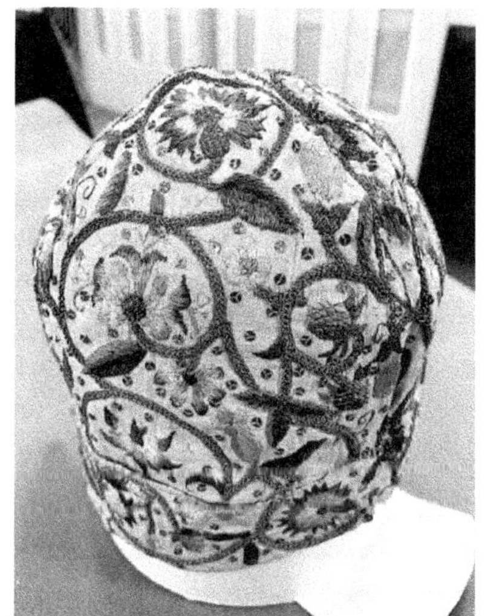

Ashmolean Museum, Oxford. Photo permission by Relics in Situ.

Figure 1.12: Women transferring patterns. Clockwise by candlelight, window light, prick and pounce, and freehand drawing, Alessandro Paganino.[10]

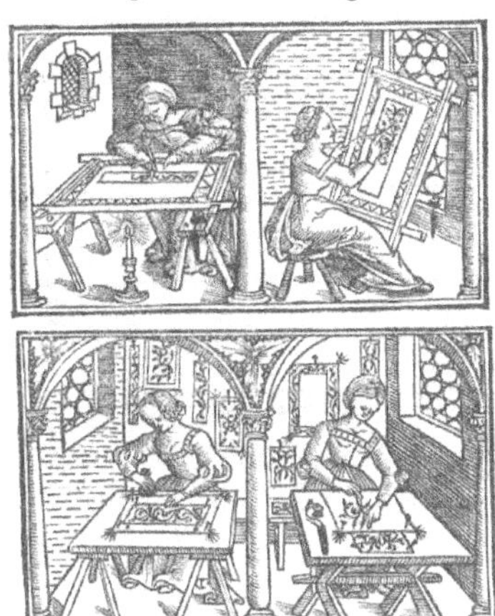

https://commons.wikimedia.org/wiki/File:Libro_quarto._De_rechami_per_elquale_se_impara_in_diuersi_modi_lordine_e_il_modo_de_recamare...Opera_noua,_page_2_(verso)_MET_DP353779.jpg (accessed December 14, 2022).

---

[10] Alessandro Paganino. Libro quarto. De rechami per elquale se impara in diuersi modi lordineil modo de recamare...Opera noua. 1532. https://archive.org/details/Paganino1532LibroQuartoMET

The patterns or images from any of these wide range of sources would be transferred to the cloth through a variety of methods, including freehand drawing, illumination with a candle or natural light, and the prick and pounce method (Figure 1.12). With this last technique, holes are pricked through an image on paper, which is then laid on the textile to be embroidered. A fine powder of charcoal (for light fabrics) or chalk (for dark fabrics) was pressed or "pounced" through the holes to transfer the outline to the fabric underneath, creating the pattern to be embroidered. This dot-to-dot image was then drawn over with a stylus or paint brush, and the powder was brushed away, leaving a complete pattern image to be covered with the needlework. There are a number of embroideries where the threads have worn away or shattered off, leaving the drawn pattern visible underneath.

Many books show evidence of having been used as a pattern, going through the pricked and pounced process with tell-tale tiny holes and charcoal smudges. A book in the Huntington Library of embroidery patterns has been pierced through, the punched dots visible on the reverse of the pattern page.[11] An herbal in the Folger Shakespeare Library shows similar distressing with holes pricked in an illustration of a tulip with charcoal lightly smudged on the paper.[12]

Patterns for embroidery were valued in and of themselves and were even given as gifts where a pattern was drawn on the fabric, which was intended to have embroidery, but it was not actually done. In *Queen Elizabeth's Wardrobe Unlock'd*, Janet Arnold notes that there were two patterns for sleeves drawn out but not yet embroidered, given as a gift to Queen Elizabeth as a part of the New Year's Rolls.[13] This type of gift would be more affordable for courtiers lower in rank and with less wealth since the embroidery would require an additional investment in money for the materials and the skill to complete.

After the pattern was transferred to the ground cloth by any method, it would be worked by the people who would complete the embroidery. These embroiderers could occupy a range of situations, starting with the fully

---

[11] John Taylor. *The Needle's Excellency*. London: James Boler. 1634. Call number 69626

[12] Crispijn van de Passe. *Hortus floridus. French. pt. 1-2 Imprimes a Vtrecht : Ches Crispian de Pas et se trouverront a Arnhem ches* Ian Ianssoon, [1615?-1617].Folger Shakespeare Library call number SB450.P2 F7 1615 Cage.

[13] Janet Arnold, ed., *Queen Elizabeth's Wardrobe Unlock'd: The Inventories of the Wardrobe of Robes Prepared in July 1600 Edited from Stowe MS 557 in the British Library, MS LR 2/121 in the Public Record Office, London, and MS V.b.72 in the Folger Shakespeare Library, Washington DC* (London New York: Routledge, 2018), 93.

professional embroiderers who were guild members and worked in a formal shop, or were commissioned to come to a large and wealthy household to work on more extensive projects. There were also people who worked in a more informal, though still professional capacity. Usually, these were women who were employed by other women to come to a house and work on projects in a domestic setting. In addition, women who lived together would work on projects either by themselves or with other members of the household, like relatives or servants.

In any of these situations, the cost of the materials ranged widely but do not seem to be prohibitive for these smaller projects. At the simplest and least expensive end, the linen thread used for picots and other edgings were readily accessible, as was the linen used for the ground cloth of the caps and coifs themselves. The silk thread for blackwork or polychrome work was imported from the continent because England was not producing silk during this time period. However, as we discussed earlier with Thomasina Walters, black silk thread was not beyond the financial reach of a girl of the middling sort as the silver and silver-gilt metal threads and embellishments, including gilt spangles, would necessarily be far costlier. This subject of the cost of embroidery materials is worthy of additional in-depth research.

It can be difficult to distinguish between the highly competent domestic and the professional needleworker due to limited documentary evidence and the fact that domestic embroiderers could, in many circumstances, have highly developed skills based on years of experience. Women were instructed in needlework from an early age and could develop a high level of competency over time. Needlework can be evaluated based on the skill and techniques used to create the object, but it is only an observational estimate. Variations in skill are indicated by uneven stitch length, variable tension, inconsistent application of the design, and sometimes lower quality materials. Professionally created needlework would presumably display a higher level and consistency of technical skill, and use of high-quality materials. Whether domestic, professional, or a combination of both, all these needleworkers drew from similar sources for patterns, and employed the same techniques for transferring those images and executing the embroidery.

Many embroidery projects could be started in one setting and finished in another. For instance, Samuel Pepys' wife, Elisabeth, worked closely with professional upholsterers to plan, design, and manage the creation of a set of hangings for her house. She did some of the embroidery work and then turned to the upholsters to finish the functional work and hang them in the house.[14]

While embroiderers would hew closely to the design sources or recurring visual motifs, they expressed some creativity through their color, material, and technique choices within the boundaries of common practice. For instance, the coiling stem design was often worked in plaited braid stitch using silver gilt thread, but could also be executed in open ladder or Ceylon stitch or a variation of those with additional wrapping threads in a show of conspicuous consumption since those used more time and materials to complete Many of the flowers were often worked in detached buttonhole stitch which could be used to create dimensionality (Figure 1.13 and Figure 1.14).

Figure 1.13: Woman's Coif detail.

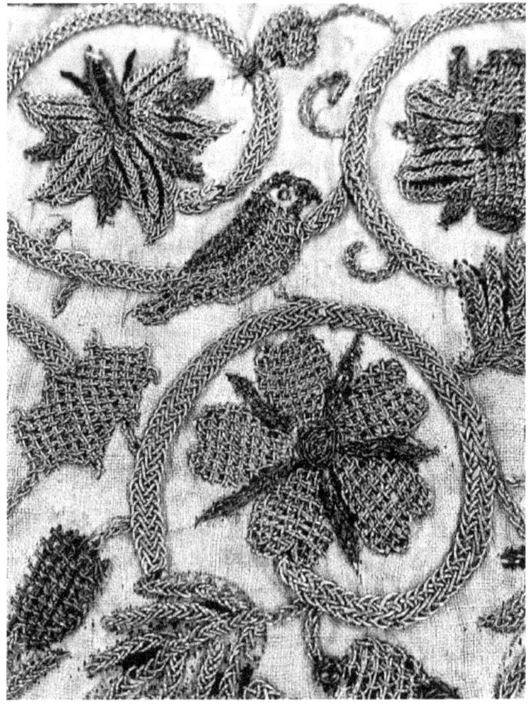

Artist Unknown.Ashmolean Museum, Oxford. Photo permission by Relics in Situ.

---

[14] Pamela Clabburn. *The National Trust Book of Furnishing Textiles.* (United Kingdom: Penguin, 1989) 75.

Figure 1.14: Woman's Coif.

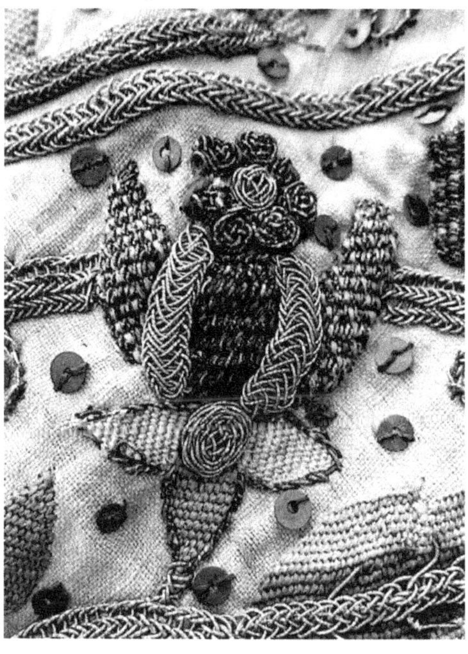

Artist Unknown. Fitzwilliam Museum, Cambridge. Photo permission by Relics in Situ.

The more challenging techniques required more time and skills and would imply that they were done by a professional or highly skilled domestic needleworker. Other caps and coifs employ simpler approaches like chain, stem, back, or straight stitches. The monochromatic red silk coif in the Victoria and Albert uses a range of less technically challenging stitches. However, the use of these simpler stitches does not always indicate a domestic embroiderer.

In addition to the embroidered images, other embellishments would sometimes be added, including spangles and lace. Spangles are silver gilt discs with a small punched hole in the middle. They varied in size and were tacked down with either two or three stitches or using a small piece of metal bullion in the center as an anchor. The lace added to the edge or brim of a cap or coif was either of white linen or metal thread bone lace. The metal thread lace could also have small teardrop-shaped spangles attached, which would quiver slightly when moved (Figure 1.15).

Figure 1.15: Man's Cap detail. Artist Unknown

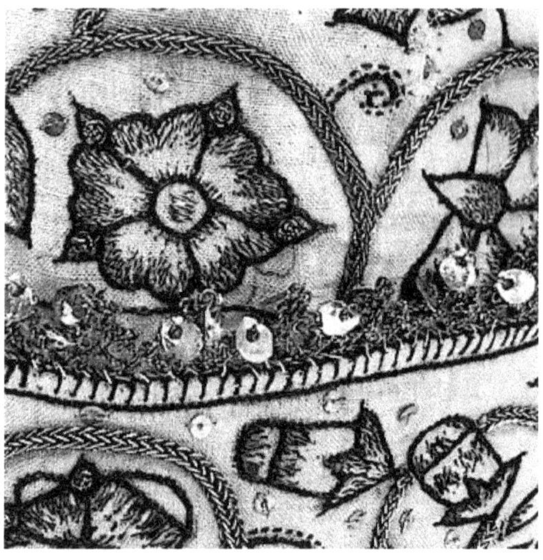

Artist Unknown. Victoria and Albert Museum, London. Photo permission by Relics in Situ.

Oftentimes, on caps and coifs, the actual size of the embroidered images can be quite small; in the case of the red silk work coif from the Victoria and Albert Museum, the figures are approximately one-inch square. Both the diminutive size as well as the exuberance of these arrangements invite the viewer to step closer to examine the detailed depictions. The visual effect of an embellished cap or coif could be appreciated at varying distances: from further away across a room, the richly colored silk and metal thread would be bright and graphically dramatic. From a midpoint, the viewer would appreciate the colors of the design and glinting spangles and lace, and when the viewer or guest was at the closest and most intimate distances, they would be able to notice the details of the embroidery itself.

Men's Embroidered Caps

When men's embroidered caps are depicted in portraiture, they are reflective of a very specific and limited group of the very wealthy who would have had the interest in, and resources to, capture their image. The man who was the subject of the painting would have specific requirements about how he wanted to be portrayed, what clothes he would be shown wearing, and the background of the setting. All of these important details created a highly cultivated image to convey a narrative of who he was and his importance in the world. A good artist would also make a conscious decision on how to paint this person, how to flatter them, and how much detail to include.

Figure 1.16: Charles Howard, 1536-1624, 1st Earl of Nottingham

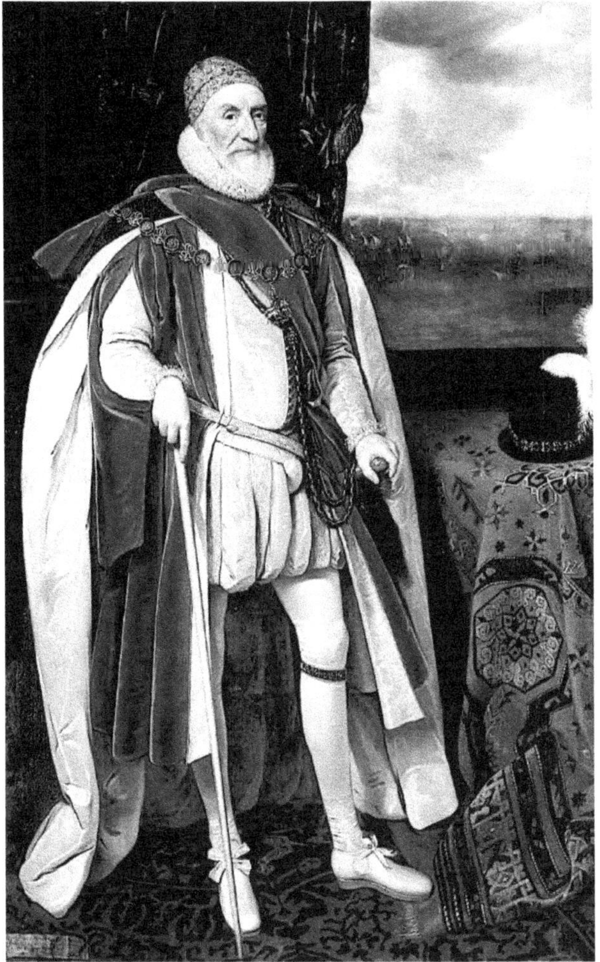

Daniel Mytens, Charles Howard, 1536-1624, 1st Earl of Nottingham, circa 1620, National Maritime Museum, London, England, File: Charles Howard (1536-1624), by Daniel Mytens.jpg," Wikimedia Commons, the free media repository, https://commons.wikimedia.org/w/index.php?title=File:Charles_Howard_(1536-1624),_by_Daniel_Mytens.jpg&oldid=712108021 (accessed January 20, 2023).

For instance, Charles Howard, first Earl of Nottingham, chose to portray himself as a wealthy man at the height of his power (Figure 1.16). He is wearing his elaborate and formal robes of state made of yards of white silk satin and red velvet, his gold and jeweled chain of state, along with white silk satin double and trunk hose, and white silk stockings, in addition to his polychrome silk and metal thread embroidered cap.[15] His noble status is communicated in every element of this portrait, including the critical inclusion of his highly embroidered cap.

Figure 1.17: Phineas Pett by Unknown artist oil on panel, circa 1612.

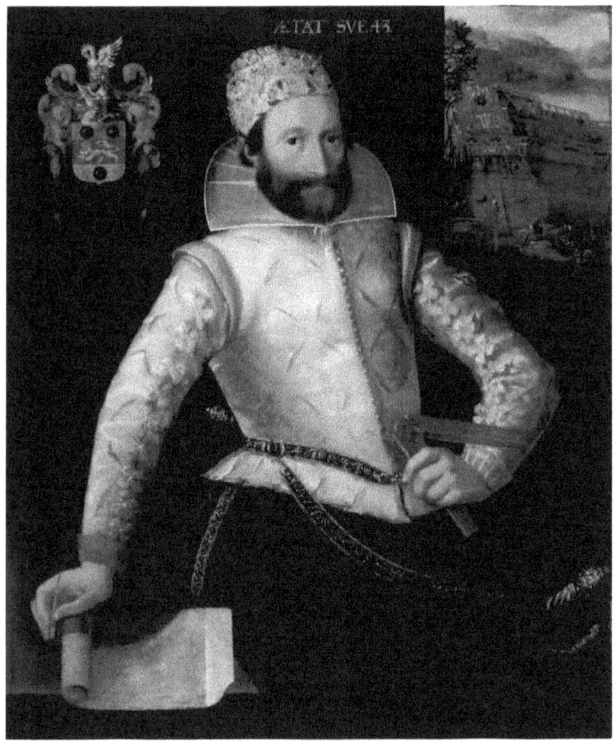

NPG 2035, National Portrait Gallery, London.

[15] Daniel Mytens, *Charles Howard, 1536-1624, 1st Earl of Nottingham,* circa 1620, National Maritime Museum, London, England, File:Charles Howard (1536-1624), by Daniel Mytens.jpg," *Wikimedia Commons, the free media repository,* https://commons.wikimedia.org/w/index.php?title=File:Charles_Howard_(1536-1624),_by_Daniel_Mytens.jpg&oldid=712108021 (accessed January 20, 2023).

Another example is the portrait of Phineas Pett when he was the Commissioner of the Navy (Figure 1.17). In the painting, Pett is wearing an impressive white silk satin doublet with embellishments of white ribbons down the sleeves and slashing details all over. He wears a dark brown trunk hose, likely of velvet or high-quality wool with gold strapwork embroidery down the side, an elaborate belt and sword scabbard, and a fine linen or silk rebato around his neck. He is also wearing a polychrome silk and metal thread embroidered cap.[16] The entirety of these details all support the assertion of wealth and power and point to his status as an elite member of society. As such, the embroidered cap reinforces this image.

When Sir John Gerrard, Lord Mayor of London, commissioned his portrait, he also chose to portray himself as a man of wealth and importance (Figure 1.18). Sir John is wearing a long coat of black with gold embellishments, a black doublet, and hose, and an elaborate white ruff at his neck edged with needle lace. Importantly, he is wearing an elaborately embroidered cap of polychrome silk and metal thread.[17] These details in the portrait, as well as the fact of the portrait itself, clearly argue that this man is of elite status in the upper echelons of power and wealth. The elaborately embroidered cap is a key part of this presentation.

All of these portraits depict men of elevated station and power who consciously included their elaborate and expensive clothing, accouterment of office or achievement, and beautifully embroidered caps. All of these men are also in interior settings, the only situations in which embroidered caps are shown.

It is important to note that while men's embroidered caps were referred to as nightcaps in contemporary documents, this does not mean they were worn to sleep in. Neither the Earl of Nottingham nor the Lord Mayor of London were wearing their robes of state or embroidered cap to bed. Beyond the practical aspect of the discomfort of sleeping with a stiff and highly textured cap, the expensive embroidery would have been damaged, and the investment in a luxury good would have been destroyed.

---

[16] Unknown, *Phineas Pett*, circa 1612, National Portrait Gallery, London, England.

[17] Daniel Mytens, Sir John Garrard (c.1546–1625), Lord Mayor of London, 1601, Guildhall Art Gallery, London, England, https://artuk.org/discover/artworks/sir-john-garrard-c-15461625-lord-mayor-of-london-1601-51385, (accessed January 20, 2023).

Figure 1.18: Sir John Garrard (c.1546–1625), Lord Mayor of London (1601)

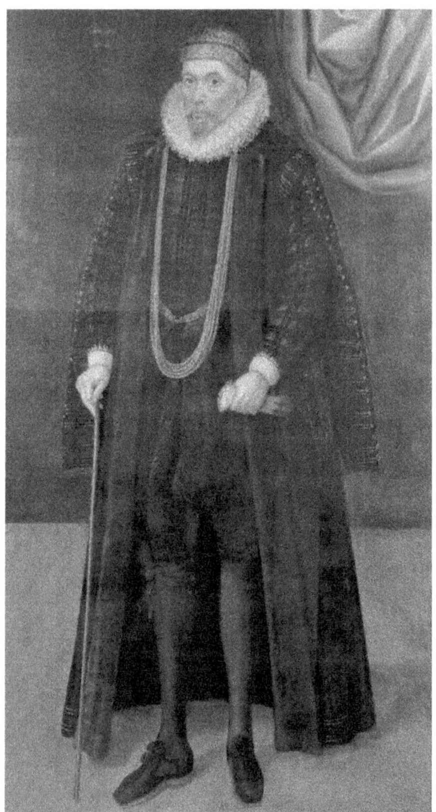

Daniel Mytens. Guildhall Art Gallery, London. https://artuk.org/discover/artworks/sir-john-garrard-c-15461625-lord-mayor-of-london-1601-51385, (accessed January 20, 2023).

Men's caps are relatively uniform in their construction, as evidenced by the visual record, extant caps, as well as patterns for construction. One of the most significant pattern sources for caps, as well as a range of other decorative applications, are the Trevelyon Manuscripts, of which three slightly different versions, written in 1603, 1608, and 1616, exist today. Thomas Trevelyon, who was most likely a draftsman, created these manuscripts as commonplace books or miscellanies. They cover a wide variety of information, including over one hundred pages of embroidery patterns, many of which are explicitly for men's caps. The significance of the Trevelyon Miscellanies, especially the 1608 and 1616 manuscripts, is that they place embroidery patterns on a par with the other information in this book, which includes rulers of England, biblical prayers, planting seasons, classical stories, etc.

The 1608 Miscellany in the Folger Shakespeare Library collection includes several illustrations of a cowslip, flower, and a man's cap in the Museum of Fine Arts Boston includes the same flower in another garden-influenced design.[18] On that cap, the petals and center body of the embroidered flower have been worked in silver gilt thread, which has tarnished, and the black silk thread of the body of the flower has shattered due to the brittleness of the iron mordant in the dye. The key elements of the flower on the cap undeniably follow the pattern of the flower in the drawing. This type of wear is unfortunate but quite common, and it allows a glimpse of the application of the pattern underneath.

Figure 1.19: Man's Cap Pattern

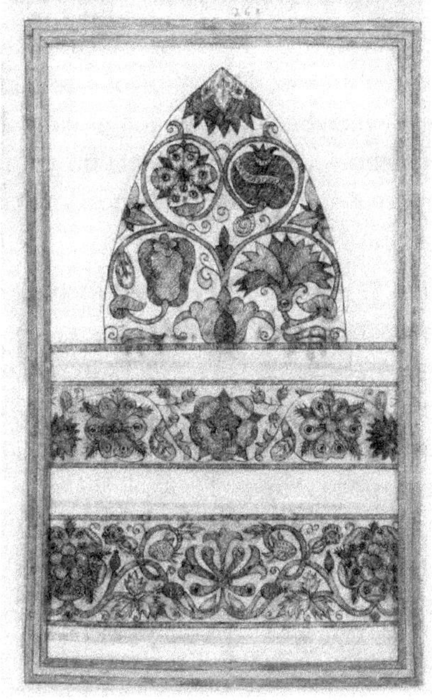

https://luna.folger.edu/luna/servlet/detail/FOLGERCM1~6~6~7033~100663:Trevelyon-Miscellany-of-1608?qvq=q:call_number%3D%22V.b.232%22&mi=482&trs=596 (accessed January 17, 2023).

---

[18] Unknown. Man's Cap, 1625, linen with silk and metal thread, Museum of Fine Arts Boston, Boston, Massachusetts. https://collections.mfa.org/objects/116887 (accessed January 22, 2023).

The Trevelyon man's cap patterns are drawn with the distinctive peak design, representing a single panel that will make up into one of four repeating sections (Figure 1.19). The rectangular designs along the bottom of the pattern were intended to be the decorative cap band. The patterns for the cap bands were not necessarily coordinated to the panel above them but intended to provide a variety of design options for the maker.

The Victoria and Albert Museum has an almost completed man's cap where the pattern was drawn on a piece of linen, with the blackwork silk embroidery completed.[19] The finished needlework was not cut out from the ground cloth or sewn up, leaving the final cap uncompleted and usefully illustrating the steps in the construction process.

Women's Coifs

Women's embroidered coifs are similar to men's caps in that they were also elaborate status symbols worn only indoors, though their structure and how they were worn was quite different. The shape of a coif laid flat is rectangular with a straight top edge (which becomes the main seam) and a slightly curved bottom edge (which becomes the gathered section worn at the base of the skull). The sides cut in curves and, when made up, form a curved shape framing the face of the wearer.

Interestingly, while the Trevelyon Miscellanies included patterns that were explicitly for men's caps, they did not have designs laid out specifically for women's coifs, though there are many pages that are entirely repeating patterns. Since a coif pattern is a modified rectangle, it could easily be adapted to the repeating patterns in the miscellany. In fact, the 1616 Trevelyon manuscript includes a stepped repeat of holly leaves and berries on an entire page, which exactly matches an embroidered coif in the collection of Embroiderers' Guild UK (Figure 1.20).

This coif, which has been completely embroidered but is laid flat, not sewn up to wear, is another example of a coiling stem and garden motif. The stem is embroidered with metal thread in a plaited braid stitch with some smaller tendrils in chain stitch. The flowers, birds, and insects are created using

---

[19] Unknown, Nightcap, circa 1600, linen with silk thread, Victoria and Albert Museum, London, England, https://collections.vam.ac.uk/item/O319540/nightcap-unknown/ (accessed January 23, 2023).

detached buttonhole stitch. These techniques were all very typical of this style of needlework on caps and coifs, as well as other types of clothes.

Figure 1.20: Woman's Coif with Holly Pattern

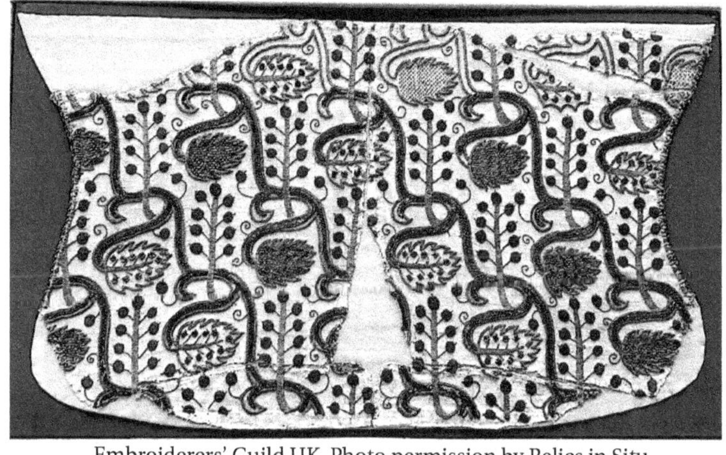

Embroiderers' Guild UK. Photo permission by Relics in Situ.

Figure 1.21: Woman's Coif

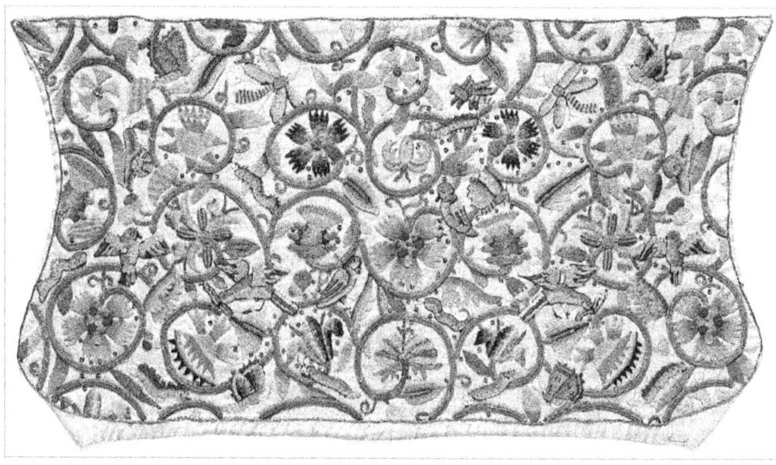

https://commons.wikimedia.org/wiki/File:Coif_MET_DP264182.jpg (accessed January 26, 2023).

Once assembled, the coif is dependent on the wearer's hair arrangement to fit securely. Women's hair was grown long and would be braided, plaited, or twisted around at the back of the head and secured with ribbon or woven strings (called tape during this time period). After the hair was bound up, the coif was placed on the head and cinched around the taped hair to create its unique silhouette.

Figure 1.22: Assembled Woman's coif

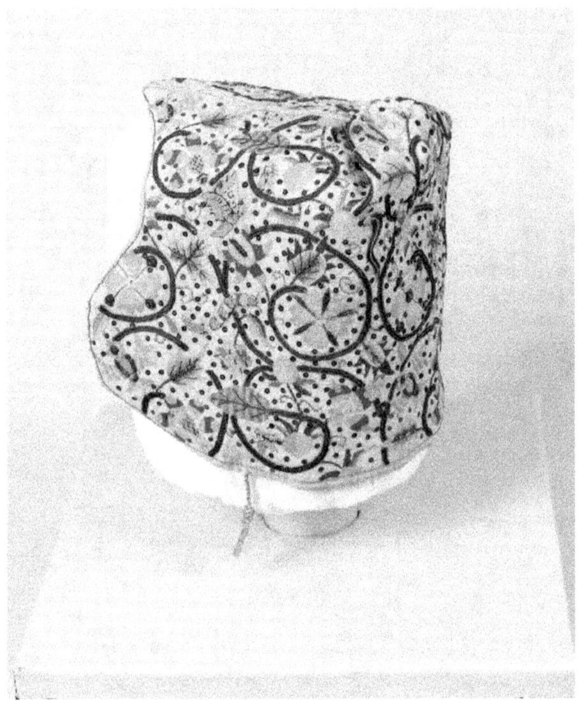

https://commons.wikimedia.org/wiki/File:Coif_(England),_late_16th%E2%80%93early_17th_century_(CH_18445167).jpg (accessed January 26, 2023).

A small number of extant embroidered coifs have a matching "forehead cloth," which is a triangular piece with tapes at two of the points and was assumed to tie at the base of the skull. There are even fewer examples in the visual record of a coif being worn with what might be interpreted as a forehead cloth, where only a small portion of that cloth is visible because it is underneath the coif. These illustrations are only of plain linen, not of embroidered coifs. Janet Arnold makes the supposition that the forehead cloth was worn during illness, from a contemporary source writing about how both Irish and English women wore them when they were ailing.[20]

While most textiles tend to be used, reused, handed down, and repurposed, a significant number of embroidered men's caps and women's coifs exist in collections today. It is possible that they were put away, saved or forgotten, because they are both beautiful and small. Even as this type of needlework embellishment fell out of fashion, it must have still been appreciated for its aesthetic qualities or, possibly more likely, because these objects were so small, there was not enough actual material to be made into another item, and they were put away and forgotten.

Figure 1.23: Joan Stint, Mrs. George Evelyn (1550-1613)

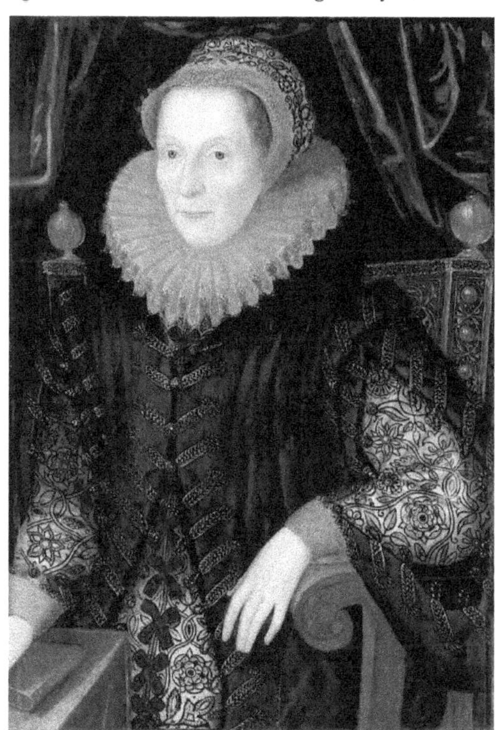

https://commons.wikimedia.org/wiki/File:Attributed_to_John_Bettes_the_Younger_Portrait_of_Joan_Stint,_Mrs_George_Evelyn_(1550-1613).jpg#file (accessed January 31, 2023).

[20] Janet Arnold, *Queen Elizabeth's Wardrobe Unlock'd. Queen Elizabeth's Wardrobe Unlock'd.* 48-49.

In conclusion, needle worked head coverings, caps, and coifs were more than just functional items of clothing. The added embroidery represented a purposeful attempt to assert a physical manifestation of wealth and power, both important signifiers in an extremely hierarchical society. These caps and coifs became status symbols precisely because they were embellished. And that embellishment was derived from a variety of sources, including published patterns, herbals, natural histories, and emblem books.

These patterns and illustrations, as well the embroideries themselves, all follow common characteristics that made these flowers, printed and needle worked, very emblematic, which anyone from this time period would have immediately recognized. Indeed, they were part of a shared language of visual motifs. The needle work done on these caps and coifs represents an economic network that supplied silver-gilt thread and spangles, silk thread from Europe, steel needles, first imported to, and then produced in England, and the time and skill of the embroiderers, whether domestic or professional. In other words, a hat is never just a hat.

Bibliography

Arnold, Janet. *Queen Elizabeth's Wardrobe Unlock'd*, W.S. Maney & Sons Ltd., Leeds UK 1988.

Clabburn, Pamela. *The National Trust Book of Furnishing Textiles.* United Kingdom: Penguin, 1989.

Dorman, Thomas. "The Sandwich Book of Orphans." *Archaeologia Cantiana* 16 (1886): 179-206.

Goodman, Ruth. *How to Be a Tudor: a Dawn-to-Dusk Guide to Tudor Life.* First American edition. New York: Liveright Publishing Corporation, a division of W.W. Norton & Company, 2016.

Mikhaila, Ninya and Dr. Jane Malcolm-Davies. *The Tudor Tailor: Reconstructing Sixteenth-Century Dress.* Hollywood: Costume and Fashion Press, 2006.

Morrall, Andrew and Melinda Watt. *English embroidery from the Metropolitan Museum of Art, 1580-1700: 'twixt art and nature.* New York: The Bard Graduate Center for Studies in the Decorative Arts, Design, and Culture; The Metropolitan Museum of Art; Yale UP 2008.

North, Susan. "An Instrument of profit, pleasure and of ornament": Embroidered Tudor and Jacobean Dress Accessories," in *English embroidery from the Metropolitan Museum of Art, 1580-1700: 'twixt art and nature*, ed. Andrew Morrall and Melinda Watt (New Haven and London: Yale UP, 2006).

Paganino, Alessandro. *Libro quarto. De rechami per elquale se impara in diuersi modi lordineil modo de recamare...Opera noua.* 1532. Venice: Paganino, Paganini, & Paganino, Alessandro, 1532. https://archive.org/details/Paganino1532LibroQuartoMET (accessed December 14, 2022).

Passe, Crispijn van de. *Jardin de Fleurs, Contenant Soy Les Plus Rare et Plus Excellentes Fleurs Que Pour le Present les Amateurs Dicelles Tiennent en Grande Estime et Dignite. 1593.* Imprimes a Vtrecht : Ches Crispian de Pas et se trouverront a Arnhem ches Ian Ianssoon, [1615?-1617]. Folger Shakespeare Library, call number SB450.P2 F7 1615 Cage.

Shorleyker, Richard. *A Schole-house, for the Needle,* United Kingdom: [Pinted [sic] in Shoe-lane, at the signe of the Faulcon, by Richard Shorleyker.], 1632.

Speelberg, Femke. "Fashion & Virtue: Textile Patterns and the Print Revolution 1520–1620." Bulletin - Metropolitan Museum of Art 73, no. 2 (2015).

Stent, Peter. *A Book of flowers, fruits, beasts, birds, and flies : seventeenth-century patterns for embroiderers printed and sold by Peter Stent.* Austin: Curious Works Press, 1995.

Taylor, John. *The Needles Excellency: A New Booke wherin are diuers Armirable Workes wrought with the Needle.* London; James Baler, 1631.

Tolley, Thomas, "Visual Culture." In *Gentry Culture in Late-Medieval England,* edited by Raduca Radelescu and Alison Truelove, 167-182. Manchester: Manchester UP, 2005.

Trevelyon, Thomas. *Trevelyon Miscellany of 1608* [manuscript]. Folger Shakespeare Library, accessed December 15, 2022, https://luna.folger.edu/luna/servlet/view/search?q=call_number=%22V.b.232%22 (accessed January 17, 2023).

Tagliente, Giovanni Antonio. *Opera nuova che insegna alle donne a cusire, a racammare e a disegnar a ciascuno Et la ditta opera sara di grande utilita ad ogni artista per esser il disegno ad ogniuno necessario laqual e ititolata estempio di recamini : Stampato in Vineggia per Giovan Antonio & i fratelli da Sabbio MDXXX.* 1530. Vineggia: Giovan Antiono & Brothers, 1530. https://archive.org/details/tagliente1530operabnfbtv1b10548051/page/n27/mode/2up. (Accessed December 14, 2022).

Chapter 2

In It to Win It: The Evolution of Fightwear in Mixed Martial Arts Combat Sports

Jeremiah Snyder

American InterContinental University

Abstract: The historical concept of fight, physical encounter, combat, or bout and its connection with related-attire in the context of mixed martial arts (MMA) combat sports. MMA has changed significantly since its inception as it has grown in popularity, specifically with regard to the fightwear that is worn by mixed martial artists, especially those worn by fighters in the Ultimate Fighting Championship promotion since its formation in 1993. The choice of fightwear by the fighter could dramatically alter the way combatants engaged with each other. Today, fightwear is regulated by the promotion and the sanctioning body, whether it be an individual state commission or a nation's regulating body. The evolution of fight costumes demonstrates not only the utility of the attire but also the changing rules due to a variety of influences external to the fighter's preference, such as the fight promotors, the governing commission, and the fans.

Keywords: American kickboxing, Bellator, Brazilian jiu-jitsu, Catch wrestling, Fightwear, Kempo karate, Mixed Martial Arts, Savat, Shoot wrestling, Sumo, tae kwon do, Venum

***

For the Ultimate Fighting Championship 133, Dennis Hallman stepped into the octagon to face Brian Ebersal on 6 August 2011 for the main card's final event. Both were experienced fighters, so it was thought by many that this fight would be the most exciting on the card, which is why it was scheduled at the end of the night. The fight was exciting although short: Ebersal got Hallman to the ground, then mounted him. Once Ebersal was on top of Hallman in a full mount, Ebersal proceeded to punch the man beneath him in the face. The referee put an end to the match at four-minutes twenty-eight seconds into the first round. After the fight, UFC president Dana White was livid, but not because the evening's top fight ended so quickly. Rather, he was upset because Hallman entered the octagon wearing what was essentially a blue speedo. As White said in an interview following the night's events, "I've never been so embarrassed being in the UFC."[1] Hallman would get another chance to fight for White and the UFC fans, seeing action in UFC 140, but he did not wear spandex swimwear for that fight. At any rate, UFC 140 would be the last time Hallman would grace the cage with his presence.

The controversy Hallman caused by wearing his fight attire for UFC 133 had lasting reverberations in the UFC as both fans and White were upset, even shocked, with what Hallman had chosen. Although this fight costume was similar to what UFC legends Ken Shamrock and Dan Severn had worn into the octagon during the 1990s and early 2000s when they donned their spandex wrestling briefs, fightwear people regularly saw on the likes of Hulk Hogan, The Ultimate Warrior, or Ric Flair in World Wrestling Federation or World Championship Wrestling matches, by 2011 such attire was no longer worn in the octagon. It had become passé, archaic, something from a bygone era where the fighters were remembered fondly, but their fight costumes were not. However, the rules on fightwear in the earliest days of the UFC were not enforced to the letter; fighters could wear whatever they wanted. Then, from about UFC 30 to UFC 133, or roughly 2001 to 2011, fighters could wear shorts of various styles with their sponsors' advertisements emblazoned on them. Yet, it was Hallman's speedo fiasco that would encourage White to seek out standardized fight attire.

Sanctioned, licensed mixed martial arts combat sports are some of the most popular events taking place around the world today. Similar to all sports, MMA has changed significantly since its inception as it has grown in popularity, specifically with regard to the fightwear, or costumes, that mixed martial artists wear. Fightwear worn by fighters in the Ultimate Fighting Championship promotion since its formation in 1993 has evolved significantly since the promotion began. It was in the first UFC fight card where combatants could wear anything they wanted, such as full *keikogi* or less, including lycra or

---

[1] Matt Juul, "Dennis Hallman's Shorts: Dana White Speaks About Speedo & More," *Bleacher Report*, August 8, 2011, https://bleacherreport.com/articles/796989-ufc-133-hallman-speaks-out-about-speedo-arm-injury.

spandex wrestling singlets or even wrestling briefs. The lycra and spandex wrestling singlets were often seen in the World Wrestling Federation, now known as World Wrestling Entertainment, Inc., or seen in World Championship Wrestling, which was acquired by the WWE in 2001. The choice of fightwear by the fighter might not only dramatically alter the way combatants engage with each other but also provide a mixture of fight costumes for each event.

Today, fightwear is regulated by the promotion and the sanctioning body, whether it be an individual state commission or a nation's regulating body. In the case of the UFC, both the promotion as well as the sanctioning body, which is the National Association of Boxing Commissions, regulate fightwear from the clothing the fighters put on to the gloves they wear, as well as their groin protection and their mouthguards. All of these regulations are intended to protect each fighter from unnecessary harm while considering the demands of the live and televised audiences, among other demands. As a result, fighters participating in the sport of MMA today are restricted in what they can wear for the fight.

The evolution of fight costumes is an area that has been largely overlooked by those writing about the sport or discussing it. Much has been said about the various fighting styles involved in the sport of mixed martial arts. Additionally, much has been said about the injuries fighters incur for being involved in the sport, and much has been said about the business itself. What has been said about fight costumes in MMA, though, has been relegated to the business discussion of the sport and thus focuses mostly on how promotions, fighters, and clothing companies make or lose money because of the contracts signed between each of them. Although this is an interesting and valuable area of scholarship, it is but one aspect of the complex development of fight attire in MMA. Therefore, the evolution of fight costumes is interesting as it demonstrates the utility of the attire, which each fighter considers before they engage in combat with their opponent. This study also shows how changing rule sets due to a variety of influences external to the fighter's preferences affected fighter costumes. Counted among these external influences are the demands of the fight promotors of the MMA organization, the governing commission, and the fans. Due to both these personal and external influences, over time, fighters chose to, or had to, alter what they wore into the octagon.

The Ultimate Fighting Championship celebrated its 29-year anniversary on 11 November 2022. The first mainstream promotion to offer mixed martial arts combat sports to the masses via ticketed sales and television, the UFC has grown into a global phenomenon, making its name and MMA common in household conversations. Many other MMA promotions have come into being since the UFC started, such as PRIDE Fighting Championships, which started in 1997 and was closely associated with the Yakuza crime syndicate of Japan, thus leading to the demise of the promotion. Bellator Fighting Championships, now Bellator MMA, was founded in 2007 in Chicago, Illinois, but the headquarters are now in Hollywood, California. ONE Championship started in 2011 and is based in Singapore, boasting fight cards that are available to view in over 170 countries, and that can be seen by over 2 billion people live as the action happens.[2] ONE Championship, the UFC, and Bellator MMA are considered the most popular by the number of viewers who watch their events, either live at the arena or on TV, and the by the fighters they are able to sign, but there are many other international and regional MMA organizations. The first to take the sport of MMA mainstream, though, was the Ultimate Fighting Championship. It is in the first several sanctioned UFC fights that a variety of pure martial arts styles and their associated fight costumes can be found. As PRIDE, Bellator MMA, and ONE Championship both started after the UFC, the changes in fightwear were already well underway as the rules governing the sport from the earliest days to when these promotions began had already undergone significant changes. Therefore, this history of the evolution of MMA fight attire will focus on the UFC and the changes that came about as a result of various regulation changes, as well as the sport of MMA becoming more popular over the years since the start of the UFC in 1993.

Although many works have covered the beginning of the Ultimate Fighting Championship, and they all differ depending on who is telling the story, the majority of the information is the same with all those who were there at the start. In summary, the UFC started because the Gracie family of Brazil, who had been practicing their particular form of Japanese jiu-jitsu since Carlos Gracie learned it from Mitsuyo Maeda in the 1920s, wanted to prove that their form of the martial art was the superior form.[3] Carlos taught his brother Helio, and soon after, the two started a dojo to teach others. Then, Gracie jiu-jitsu took Rio de Janeiro by storm. In 1978, Helio's son Rorian (pronounced *H*orian) moved to Torrance, California, to start teaching Gracie jiu-jitsu out of his garage.[4] When

---

[2] "About One," One Championship, accessed February 10, 2023, https://www.onefc.com/about-us/.

[3] "Grand Master Carlos Gracie: The Beginning of Everything," Rilion Gracie Jiu-Jitsu, accessed December 30, 2021, https://www.riliongracie.com/carlos-gracie/.

[4] "UFC founder Rorion Gracie talks early UFC experience (Part 2/2)," Sherdog.com, Evolve Media, December 22, 2016, https://www.youtube.com/watch?v=BOvYRsUD4AQ&ab_channel=Sherdog.com.

Art Davie met Rorian in the early 1990s at Rorian's newly established Gracie Jiu-Jitsu Academy, they put together the *Gracie in Action* VCR tapes.[5] Rorian was trying to sell the grappling martial art developed and practiced by his family to the masses, just as his father and uncle had done in Brazil. Specifically, he wanted to sell his family's Brazilian jiu-jitsu as the best grappling art form that everyone could use to defend themselves against potential aggressors in real-world situations. This is how the Gracie Challenge came to the United States after it had been utilized to great effect by Helio in Brazil to get the better of many martial artists. Rorian's Gracie Challenge offered $100,000 to anyone who could defeat Rorian or one of his brothers with any fighting style in any place. However, the fight had to be in front of a camera. Yet, these stipulations were never strictly adhered to, especially the $100,000 purse, as, for the Gracies, defending their honor and proving that their fighting style was superior always took precedence over money. By the time Davie came along with his idea for a best-of-the-best martial artist matchup, many different fighters had already fallen to the Gracies in Torrance. So, Rorian initially refused Davie's proposition to have his challenge become a money making, televised enterprise.

Rorian's mind changed when financial investors in the form of Semaphore Entertainment Group supported this notion, and the Ultimate Fighting Championship came to be. Davie and Rorian wanted to protect their original idea of a "no holds barred" fighting championship, so they founded W.O.W. Promotions (which stands for War of the Worlds) before signing the contract with the managing interests behind SEG, who were Bob Meyrowitz, Campbell McLaren, Michael Abramson, and Michael Pillot.[6] The Ultimate Fighting Championship was to operate under nearly the same premise as the Gracie Challenge: the best fighter representing the best fighting style would win $50,000 after defeating several other fighters. The competition would be a grand prix tournament matchup that would pit one fighter against another, one martial arts style against the other, in a single night. With everyone on board and a financial backer in place, UFC 1 started to take shape.

Once the UFC had been created and it had some financial support, a location was needed to host the event. Such a location was found in Denver, Colorado. In fact,

---

[5] Joe Rogan and "Big" John McCarthy, "JRE MMA Show #26 with Big John McCarthy," May 15, 2018, in *Joe Rogan Experience*, produced by Jamie Vernon, podcast, video and MP3 audio, 2:26:12, https://open.spotify.com/episode/277VQ10aGB2fGbOGKnVI6u.

[6] Art Davie, *Is this Legal? The Inside Story of the First UFC From the Man Who Created It*, with Sean Wheelock (Olathe, KS: Ascend Books, 2014), 160.

both UFC 1: The Ultimate!, which would become known as UFC 1: The Beginning later, and UFC 2: No Way Out were hosted in Denver. UFC 1: The Ultimate! was held at McNichols Sports Arena on 12 November 1993, and the follow-up event was held at Mammoth Gardens on 11 March 1994. One of the reasons the first two UFCs were held in Denver is because, at the time, the state did not have a sports commission that oversaw striking events like this.[7] States with commissions that had regulations for striking and grappling contests were likely to bar mixed events such as the UFC. However, the governor of Colorado and the mayor of Denver were both willing to allow the events to take place. As a result, the first two UFCs took place in Colorado, and several afterward took place in states where state governments or just city governments sanctioned the events.

Indeed, to give the sport and the UFC the guise of legitimacy, Davie created the International Fight Council in 1993, prior to the first event. Rorion was the commissioner of this "paper" sanctioning body, and it was the IFC that approved the rules of the UFC's fights until further intervention. That Colorado did not have a commission to oversee this event is important as the rules governing these first UFC events are the rules created by the promotion itself, not the rules of any regulating body. Therefore, W.O.W. Promotions wrote the rules that governed the actions of the fighters rather than a recognized regulating organization such as the Association of Boxing Commissions.

There are some discrepancies between the rules for the first UFC depending on whether it is Art Davie's or Campbell McLaren's account that should be accepted. Both are co-founders of the UFC, but Davie is the co-founder of W.O.W. Promotions with Rorion, and it is these two who also headed the IFC. The rules according to McLaren are found on his Twitter account.[8] The directives according to Davie are found on page 179 of his book, *Is This Legal?*, and these are given precedent in this study since Davie is more instrumental in the organization of these early fights. The regulations that are of greatest interest, then, are C, F, and G, and Davie writes them as:

> C. Fighters wear clothing according to their style, as long as it complies with IFC rules. Rorian Gracie, IFC commissioner and the referees to inspect each fighter prior to event.

---

[7] Mark Kriegel, "Jim Brown is shilling for sick thrills," *The Evening Sun*, March 8, 1994, 8C.

[8] Campbell McLaren (@campbellcombate), ".@nicklembo I said "No rules but there were some. Page from UFC 1 rule book. #UFCarchives #originalUFC #Combate." Twitter, May 14, 2014, https://twitter.com/campbellcombate/status/466590010771529728.

F. Target areas for all strikes include head and body with the exception of the eyes and groin.
G. 6- or 8-ounce boxing gloves or Kempo gloves are optional if a fighter's art employs closed fist strikes to the face and head, otherwise bare knuckles are permitted.
  1. Taping of wrist must end one inch away from knuckle. Tape should be placed on top of wraps.
  2. Shoes-boxing or wrestling shoes allowed if the fighter does not use any kicking.
  4. No shin guards or arm pads.[9]

These rules require some analysis in order to understand why fighters wore the fight costumes they wore in UFC 1. It is apparent early on that not all fighting styles have easily identifiable fightwear, such as *gis* or boxing shorts. Other fighting styles, such as sumo, might not have the fightwear the fighter wants to wear for UFC fights. Therefore, Rule C creates a problem for some combatants before the bouts even begin. Rule F explicitly states that the groin and eyes are not to be targeted by strikes. Contestants would challenge this with Rorian and Davie prior to UFC 1, and the rule would be broken shortly thereafter in the second bout of the inaugural contest. Also, in the fighter meeting that took place the night before the event, it was asked if groin protection or mouth guards could be worn. Rorian replied that both could be worn or not at a fighter's discretion.[10] In addition to all this, looking at Rule G and watching the first 10 UFC events, it can be seen that many fighters did not wear gloves of any sort, although they had the option to.

Once the rules were established for the first UFC contest, they were almost immediately broken or disregarded. Teila Tuli, the six-foot two-inch tall, 410-pound fighter who specialized in sumo, chose not to wear a *mawashi*, or the cloth wrapped around the sumo wrestler's hips and groin, for his UFC 1 match. Tuli thought this an unacceptable option for a cage brawl. In fact, he did not even bother to bring his *mawashi* with him from Hawaii to Colorado. However, as boxing shorts or other fight gear in size 60 could not be found the day before the fight in Denver, Tuli had to buy traditional Samoan attire somewhere in the Mile High City for his fight.[11] In not donning his *mawashi*, though, Tuli

---

[9] Davie, *Is this Legal?*, 179.

[10] Davie, *Is this Legal?*, 207 – 208.

[11] Davie, *Is this Legal?*, 215.

disregarded Rule C. Neither Rorian nor Davie said anything to him about it, and no fighter at UFC 1 is known to have complained. Other competitors did the same as Tuli with regard to the octagon mandates in the first UFC event. Therefore, it can be concluded that the IFC rules were more like guidelines.

With Tuli's decision to forgo his *mawashi*, when UFC 1 began that November night in 1993, most people in attendance or watching at home through pay-per-view might not have recognized what the sumo wrestler from Hawaii was wearing. Indeed, the commentators sitting ringside – Bill Wallace, Jim Brown, and Kathy Long – were not familiar with the fight costume, with Long asking what Tuli was wearing as he entered the arena. Wallace replied, "It's a Samoan type of a gown."[12] Although not entirely incorrect, what Tuli was wearing was a sarong, or an *ie lavalava*. According to the Museum of New Zealand, the *ie lavalava* has been worn in Samoa since the 1800s, if not earlier.[13] Originally made of siapo (barkcloth), the *ie lavalava* is worn about the waist, and a separate piece is also worn around the torso, or a very long garment can be worn wrapped just underneath the armpits around the chest. Tuli wore two garments while walking to the octagon: one segment of cloth was wrapped around his waist and extended to his knees while he held the other segment wrapped around his shoulders. In addition to the *ie lavalava*, Tuli wore a light brown beanie while walking to the fight cage. Just before the fighter introductions were complete, Tuli removed the beanie from his head and the cloth from about his shoulders, leaving the single piece wrapped about his waist for his cage fight with Gerard Gordeau. Furthermore, Tuli had his wrists and thumb taped to just below the interphalangeal joint, or the lowest knuckle of his thumb. The tape stretched across the rest of his hand and palm but stopped one inch below the knuckles of his four fingers, leaving them exposed.

Tuli's *ie lavalava* was both traditional and modern. Patterns of *ie lavalavas* are often described in the historical documents of Western sources as being typically monochromatic. Yet, as different technology and types of cloth reached the Polynesian Islands, the patterns became more diverse. Shapes and varying colors were added in order to make the *ie lavalavas* more appealing and eye-catching. Therefore, the pattern seen on Tuli's *ie lavalava* fight costume is

---

[12] *UFC 1: The Beginning*, directed by Mark Lucas (1993; Las Vegas, NV: Zuffa, LLC., 2013), DVD.

[13] "ie lavalava 'PUMA' (cloth wrap around)," accessed January 5, 2022, cotton cloth, 1115mm (height), 1750mm (length), Museum of New Zealand, https://collections.tepapa.govt.nz/object/1151647.

contemporary in that it is dynamic and covered in a single shape. The background color is a deep yellow or gold color with black rhombus shapes on top that are connected and interspersed all across the fabric. The pattern resembles that of a diamondback rattlesnake, so it is both bold and powerful.

Like Tuli, some specialized knowledge might have been required to recognize what Gerard Gordeau was wearing when he entered the octagon. The fightwear of the six-foot five-inch savate fighter from The Netherlands could have been mistaken for pajama bottoms or sweatpants. Yet, those with more experience in martial arts would realize that Gordeau was wearing white *karatedogi* pants, or *zubon*, which karate practitioners traditionally wear, something Gordeau also had a background in.[14] This particular *zubon* seemed to be longer than standard, though, in order to fit Gordeau's tall, lithe, 215 pound frame. Unlike Tuli, Gordeau's wrists and hands were not taped.

After Tuli and Gordeau came fighters with easily identifiable fight costumes. The men who appeared in the second bout had on fightwear that could be found in any gym or exercise facility in America. Both Kevin Rosier and Zane Frazier wore white athletic shorts with front pockets and white tie strings when they entered the octagon for their UFC fight against each other. Despite being purist martial artists like many others on the fight card that evening – Rosier was an American kickboxer and Frazier, a karate practitioner – neither decided to wear the clothing their discipline called for.

If Rosier were adhering to Rule C, he should have been in ankle length pants similar to what Gordeau was wearing. In the early 1990s, the World Kickboxing Association usually had kickboxers wear ankle length pants, padded boots, and boxing gloves when fighting.[15] Following this fight costume obligation set by the WKA, Rosier could have also worn boxing gloves. Likewise, Frazier, who specialized in Kempo karate and who had fought professionally as a kickboxer, could have worn either his *karatedogi*, or *gi*, or could have worn ankle length pants with boxing gloves.

Yet, it is unclear exactly why Rosier and Frazier showed up octagon side in gym shorts that night. Rosier passed away in 2015 and did not provide an

---

[14] Masayuki Kukan Hisataka, *Scientific Karatedo* (Rutland, VT: Charles E. Tuttle Company, 1996), 16, https://www.hoopladigital.com/play/11784540.

[15] Stefano Di Marino, *A Complete Guide to Kickboxing* (New York: Enslow Publishing, LLC., 2018), 9, https://www.hoopladigital.com/play/12172211; accord "Kickboxing 1989: Martial Arts in the 80's," Sidekickboxing.co.uk, accessed February 4, 2023, https://side kickboxing.co.uk/kickboxing-1989-martial-arts-in-the-80s/.

interview for Sherdog.com. Frazier, in an interview conducted at least two decades after UFC 1 with Sherdog.com, says that his original fightwear of kickboxing pants and boxing gloves were forbidden by Rorian in the fighter meeting the night before the event.[16] However, just moments before, in the same interview, Frazier says that he had prepared himself to wrestle and be wrestled with because he expected to fight Royce at some point in the night. Thus, while preparing for the contest in one of the Denver gyms, Frazier relates that he utilized a "ground-and-pound" style of fighting that he also used in Kempo karate tournaments. It is undeniable, though, that grappling is extremely difficult with boxing gloves on. Furthermore, Frazier claims that he was told by Rorian in the fighter meeting that Frazier's hands could not be taped, but when Frazier enters the octagon the next evening not only are his hands taped but also his ankles. Taken together, these contradictory statements make Frazier's interview less than reliable.

At any rate, rather than the traditional fightwear of their martial arts discipline, both men wore gym shorts. Rosier's were pulled up past his belly button on his six-foot four-inch, 265-pound frame. The slightly leaner, 230-pound, and slightly taller, six-foot six-inch Frazier wore his shorts below his belly button. Also, both men had their wrists and hands taped in the manner of Tuli. Additionally, Rosier is wearing a mouthguard, and Frazier might be, although it is difficult to tell watching the low-quality footage taken the night of the event. Rosier might be wearing groin protection or a hard plastic or metal oblong-shaped piece, known as a cup, that varies in length and width depending on the wearer. The cup is held in a jockstrap or tied about the person, and it is intended to protect the testicles and penis of the wearer from a strike. As already stated, it can be seen that Frazier has his ankles taped, and this gives him the look of a typical striker à la *Street Fighter* video games or *Blood Sport*, the 1988 movie starring Jean-Claude Van Damme.

When Art Jimmerson, a 196-pound boxer of some renown from Missouri, stepped into the octagon for his bout against Royce (pronounced *H*oyce) Gracie, probably everyone watching the first UFC in the McNichols Arena and at home via PPV recognized his fight attire. The boxing shorts of Jimmerson could be seen on someone like Mike Tyson, Oscar De La Hoya, or Evander Holyfield on any HBO boxing card. Jimmerson's boxing trunks were black, with

---

[16] "Zane Frazier - UFC 1 20th anniversary interview part 1/2," Sherdog.com, Evolve Media, January 9, 2017, https://www.youtube.com/watch?v=nLoWqtboP3o&list=PLo0hPpEUaQtD7bkJprbpu5Yed0rDs5oge&index=36&ab_channel=Sherdog.com.

the boxer's name embroidered in silver across the waistband. The trunks were mid-thigh in length and fit Jimmerson's fit, six-feet one-inch frame well. The boxer also had on Nike running high-tops, and he wore knee wraps for support, as knee pads were not allowed.

While Jimmerson paced back and forth during the introduction announcements, across the octagon stood the meek looking Royce at six-foot one-inch and 180 pounds. He wore the traditional *jiu-jitsu gi,* or just *gi,* which is similar to the *karatedogi.* Both Brazilian jiu-jitsu practitioners and judo practitioners wear similar *gis* every moment they are in the dojo practicing their martial art on the *tatami* mats.[17] Royce's *gi* had a thick, white cotton *uwagi,* or jacket, that covered his torso to just below the waist. His legs were covered by the aforementioned *zubon,* or white cotton pants, which were reinforced with additional fabric about the knees. A cotton belt, or *obi,* that signifies the rank of the practitioner is tied around the waist to keep the *uwagi* closed and secure. As Royce had been practicing the Brazilian jiu-jitsu developed by his father, Helio, since he was about three years old, he wore a black colored *obi* tied around his waist that November night in 1993. This black *obi* told those who knew that Royce was a long-time dedicated pupil of this martial art and that he was near to earning the red-colored *obi* that signified the first level of mastery in the art. In short, then, the entirety of Royce's fightwear was traditional for his discipline and also communicated his status within that discipline to those who could interpret the signs. In addition to all this, Royce's hands were not taped; he did not seem to be wearing groin protection beneath his *zubon,* nor was he wearing a mouthguard. It was on Royce that fans would see a traditional martial art costume they were likely familiar with since karate martial artist Chuck Norris or *Karate Kid* star Ralph Macchio had both worn similarly fashioned *karatedogi* in their movies.

Although Royce's hands were not taped, one of Jimmerson's hands was taped, and he wore a single boxing glove on his left hand as this was his lead hand. One of the reasons Jimmerson wore a single glove was that he knew he was facing a world-class martial artist in Royce. Royce was skilled in grappling, whereas Jimmerson was skilled in striking. Therefore, Jimmerson wore the one boxing glove so that if Gracie were to grab Jimmerson's arm in a submission attempt, Jimmerson could tap-out, or show he was surrendering with his

---

[17] Garrison Wells, *Brazilian Jiu Jitsu: Ground Fighting Combat* (Minneapolis: Lerner Publications Company, 2012), 14, https://www.hoopladigital.com/play/11773517.

ungloved hand.[18] This was a wise decision by Jimmerson, who was submitted by Royce in about two minutes at UFC 1.

After Jimmerson and Royce finished their fight, it was time for Ken Shamrock and Patrick Smith to engage in combat. Along with Royce, Ken Shamrock wore fightwear reflective of his martial arts specialties, which were Pancrase and catch wrestling, also known as shoot wrestling. Pancrase is a sport and company started in Japan in 1993 by wrestlers Masakatsu Funaki and Minoru Suzuki.[19] The purpose of the promotion was to develop a style of mixed martial arts in Japan that was based on the ancient Greek martial art known as *pankration*. To the extent that this was successful in meeting this goal is open to debate, but that it was successful as both a business and fighting model is undeniable. Pancrase fights still occur today, not only in Japan but in other countries as well. Shamrock was one of the first fighters in this new endeavor, just as he was one of the first fighters in the new UFC. Indeed, Shamrock fought Masakatsu in Japan on September 21, 1993, and Masakatsu was in Shamrock's corner for the UFC 1 event in Denver a few weeks later, as was Takaku Fuke, whom Shamrock defeated on November 8, 1993.[20]

The Japanese Pancrase promotion advertised itself as a hybrid style of wrestling whose fighters employed open palm strikes, kicks to the stomach and legs, and submission holds in order to attain victory. It was here that Shamrock began to develop his style of submission grappling. It was also in Pancrase that Shamrock wore his signature fire engine red spandex briefs, as all fighters in the Pancrase Japan promotion wore spandex briefs, a color that the fighters chose. Since Shamrock always appeared as though he had just walked out of a Gold's Gym, even if were just strolling down the street in his everyday clothes, wearing

---

[18] Michael Stets, "UFC 1: Story behind Art Jimmerson and the lone boxing glove revealed," MMAMania.com, November 16, 2013, https://www.mmamania.com/2013/11/16/5109964/ufc-1-story-art-jimmerson-lone-boxing-glove-mma.

[19] "What's PANCRASE?," World Pancrase Create Inc., accessed February 9, 2023, https://www.pancrase.co.jp/en/htm/wht.html.

[20] "Ken Shamrock - UFC 1 20th Anniversary interview part 1/2," Sherdog.com, Evolve Media, January 9, 2017, https://www.youtube.com/watch?v=A1qytQBtxgk&list=PLo0hPpEUaQtD7bkJprbpu5Yed0rDs5oge&index=31&ab_channel=Sherdog.com; see also "Pancrase 3: Yes, We Are Hybrid Wrestlers 3," Tapology.com, accessed February 10, 2023, https://www.tapology.com/fightcenter/events/3651-pancrase-3-yes-we-are-hybrid-wrestlers-3.

what amounted to underwear on his six-feet, 220-pound frame made him seem all the more impressive.

At UFC 1, Shamrock wore spandex briefs that resembled those worn by his Pancrase colleagues in Japan and by many professional wrestlers performing in the World Wrestling Federation or the World Championship Wrestling matches. Many audience members watching UFC 1 would likely not know of Japanese Pancrase, but they would be familiar with American professional wrestling. Both the WWF and the WCW enjoyed being some of the most watched televised sporting events in the United States during the 1980s and 1990s.[21] Wrestling attire such as spandex or lycra briefs were worn by the immensely popular Hulk Hogan and Ric Flair, as well as the slightly lesser-known Ultimate Warrior or Randy "the Macho Man" Savage. All had their own action figures for sale at the local Toys-R-Us and other outlets, with each of them in their spandex briefs fight costumes. So, when Shamrock strode into the octagon wearing bright red spandex briefs and compression wrappings covering his knees and ankles, practically everyone watching UFC 1 recognized his fightwear as belonging to a wrestler.

Shamrock's opponent, on the other hand, wore fight attire that martial arts enthusiasts would recognize, but everyone else might confuse for simple boxing shorts. Smith was introduced as a tae kwon do practitioner, and he could have worn the traditional *dobok*, which looks much like a *gi*. Instead, he wore Muay Thai boxing shorts that were shorter than the boxing shorts of the day. In fact, Muay Thai shorts are closer in appearance to runner's shorts in that they stop above mid-thigh, and there is a small slit in the shorts on both outside seams on both legs. The purpose of this slit is to make it easier for the wearer to kick or knee their opponent, as these strikes can come up quite high in Thai boxing bouts. The word "Begin" is written in raised, red letters that appear in a yellow box of stitching, and all of this is placed on the waistband just below Smith's belly button. Some other raised red lettering appears across the front of the shorts, traveling from the lower right leg to the upper portion of the left leg, but no clear images could be found to determine what this says, nor is it possible to read it on

---

[21] Joe Martelli, "WWE's Evolution in the 1980's: What the World Is Watching," *Bleacher Report*, April 8, 2010, https://bleacherreport.com/articles/375317-what-the-world-is-watching-wwes-evolution-in-the-1980s; see also Dan Power, "WWE in the 1990s: The Most Important Decade In The Company's History?," *Bleacher Report*, February 8, 2011, https://bleacherreport.com/articles/600974-wwe-in-the-1990s-the-most-important-decade-in-the-companys-history.

the television recording. The shorts themselves are black, and Smith tied them at about his waistline on his six-foot two-inch, 217-pound body. Both fighters' wrists are taped, but not the palms of their hands. Smith is wearing a mouthguard, but it cannot be determined if Shamrock is wearing one.

From the previous description of all the fighters and their fight costumes for UFC 1, it can be determined that three contestants wore clothing according to their martial arts style or practice: Gerard Gordeau, Royce Gracie, and Ken Shamrock. Gordeau makes the cut, although he only wore *zubon* because he has a background in savate, or French kickboxing, which would require ankle length trousers for fighters in competition during the 1990s. Shamrock had experience in professional wrestling and catch wrestling, the former being "works" with predetermined outcomes, while the latter are "shoots" with no predetermined outcome. Then, just before UFC 1, Shamrock started in Japan Pancrase, a hybrid-style of shoot wrestling. Therefore, Shamrock's fire engine red spandex briefs were his work clothes wherever he fought or performed. Royce, as has already been detailed, practically grew up wearing his *gi*. Since he taught at his brother's academy, his *gi* was also his daily work attire. Furthermore, about half of the contestants wore mouthguards that night, and one certainly wore groin protection. In addition to all this, one fighter wore one glove.

There are many reasons why the fighters of UFC 1: The Ultimate! wore what the wore, but the simplest reason for each fight costume seems to be that no one knew the rules prior to their agreeing to the event. Davie states that he had been "procrastinating on putting together the rules and regulations, but as we hit mid-October, I knew it had to be done."[22] Hence, with about three weeks or less to go before the inaugural championship, Davie typed up the rules governing the bouts. It is unclear if any of the fighters knew of the regulations in the days or weeks before the event, but it is certain that all of them were made aware at the fighter meeting that took place the night before UFC 1 began. Royce might have known the regulations before this meeting as he was close to the IFC commissioner and the promotors, who just so happened to be his brother and his brother's friend. If fighters did not know the regulations until the night before, though, then it would be reasonable that most of them would not arrive in Denver with their traditional fight attire. Additionally, all the fighters knew long before arriving in Denver that this was a "no holds barred" fight where nearly anything was allowed to happen since Davie had told them this when he recruited them. With this in mind, Tuli did not want to fight in a

---

[22] Davie, *Is this Legal?*, 178.

sumo *mawashi* as he not only might be at a disadvantage compared to other fighters, but the *mawashi* might slip off, leaving him exposed before an unknown number of audience members. Furthermore, despite the rules and with the exception of Frazier, all the fighters were able to wear what they wanted and what they thought would give them an advantage over the other contestants. Going forward, this first championship set a precedent for future events, although starting with UFC 2: No Way Out, things would begin to change regarding fightwear.

Starting with UFC 2: No Way Out, the rules for each bout were simplified significantly to just no biting, no eye gouging.[23] Although there had been no complaints over fightwear in the first UFC, fighters could now wear whatever they wanted for their fights. In addition to this, strikes to the groin were now allowed per the regulations, but they had been allowed in UFC as no referee nor fighter had put a stop to a fight due to a groin strike. The simplified rule set had an immediate impact on fighter costumes and fighter protection.

Early in UFC 1, everyone saw Teila Tuli's tooth go flying into the front rows of McNichol's Arena after he was kicked in the face by Gordeau. Acting against the UFC 1 regulations, the referee stopped the fight, and Tuli lost, although he wanted to continue despite his injury. Fighters who witnessed this either backstage at McNichols or at home through PPV had to decide whether or not they would wear mouthguards if they chose to step into the octagon. Since there were no rules requiring such protection, starting with UFC 2, fighters had to make the conscious decision to add mouthguards and groin protection to their fightwear or forgo it, knowing there may be fight ending consequences.

If a fighter chooses to wear both or either, the fighter must then choose what brand or type they will wear into the octagon. Both items need to stay in place throughout the fight and protect the fighter appropriately, or the fight might be stopped due to injury. When mouthguards do not stay in place during a fight, it is the result of poor fitting or even no fitting at all. This is to say that the mouthguard has not been molded properly to the fighter's teeth and gums, so while their mouth is open to breathe, the gumshield may just fall out. Before mouthguards were mandatory, there were no stoppages for fighters not having properly fitting fighter protection equipment or other equipment. In today's UFC, just as in the past, it is the fighter's responsibility to ensure their equipment fits properly prior to the beginning of the fight. If it does not, and

[23] Rogan and McCarthy, "JRE MMA Show #26 with Big John McCarthy."

an injury occurs during the fight that results in a fight stoppage, the fighter may receive a loss on their record.

Much of what has been said of gumshields can also be said for groin protection equipment, although there are some variations to this particular type of equipment that do not apply to mouthguards. As with the mouthguard, it is the fighter's responsibility to buy their own groin protection and to ensure that it fits properly prior to the contest. Likewise with mouthguards and with the new regulations that began with UFC 2, if the groin protection becomes dislodged in any way as a result of the fighter's error and there is an injury that results in a fight stoppage, the fighter will receive a loss on their record.

There are two types of groin protection to be used for a "no-holds-barred" contest: the first option is where the groin protection is held securely in the more well-known jockstrap with a cup holder, whereas the second option is the less well-known (at least in the Western hemisphere) Muay Thai steel cup. The jockstrap is a single unit that is a waistband with a cup-holding pocket in the front that protects the genitals. Connected to this cup-holding pocket are two elastic bands that go out in opposite directions underneath the center of the groin, with one band each passing over a single buttock, where they then connect to the waistband. These elastic bands pull the cup-holding pocket backward and down so that the genitals are protected from strikes to the groin. The Muay Thai steel cup works in nearly the same fashion as the jockstrap with a cup pocket, except it is a metal groin protector, a cup that has strong but small, flat ropes or laces connected to it. There is a single rope connected at the top of the cup, and it passes through both sides of the cup, coming out in equal lengths on either side. This rope is to be wrapped several times around the fighter's waist before it is securely tied. There is also a single rope attached to the lowest hanging portion of the cup that will pass between the legs of the fighter. The fighter can tie this rope around his waist, or he can bring this rope around his waist and pass it through the rope at the top of his cup, then bring it back through his legs at the bottom of his cup. The fighter can make the ropes as loose or as tight as they want in order to secure this metal groin protector.

Even with the option to wear groin protection and a mouthguard, it is inconclusive based on the video recording of UFC 2 how many of the fighters chose to wear both or either. Of the 16 total fighters on the card for the second event, at least two contestants wore groin protection, and four wore mouthguards. All who wore these types of protective equipment had backgrounds in striking disciplines. Furthermore, it seems that none of the grapplers wore either groin protection or mouthguards. Interestingly enough, given the option to wear whatever fight outfit they wanted, the majority of the combatants chose to wear traditional fight costumes in UFC 2, with nearly all who appeared on the recording wearing the attire associated with the martial art they practiced.[24]

At UFC 3: The American Dream, held 9 September 1994 in Charlotte, North Carolina, 10 fighters, including the alternates, like in the first UFC, fought for the sold-out audience and those watching live on PPV. Similar to UFC 2, though, about half of the combatants wore traditional fightwear, whereas the other half wore something else. For example, sumo wrestler Emmanuel Yarbrough wore a *zubon* rather than a *mawashi*, and ninjitsu practitioner Steve Jennum wore gym shorts.[25] As far as could be determined from the DVD of the event, about the same number of fighters, nearly half, wore mouthguards, and about one-third wore groin protection. For this event, though, there was a significant decline in the number of fighters who taped their wrists and hands.

It cannot be determined from extant sources why this is so. There does not seem to be any advantage to not taping wrists and hands. Rather, there is a disadvantage in doing this as the taping of hands and wrists provides additional support to the structure of these areas. Therefore, when strikes land on an opponent, they land harder with more damage to the opponent and less damage to the hands and wrists of the striker. So, it would seem that more fighters would want to utilize this advantage rather than not. Yet, for UFC 3, evidence suggests that with almost an even number of strikers and grapplers, a significant number of participants chose to forego the taping of their wrists and hands.

However, it is worth noting that since the rules had been simplified, other advantages were utilized for the first time, with both making lasting impacts on the sport. Wrestling shoes were worn in the octagon, with Ken Shamrock making a return to the event and donning a pair. He is the first to do so. Other fighters will take note, and, as a result, there will be an increase in the use of footwear in future UFCs. Furthermore, Shamrock fought Felix Lee Mitchell, a kickboxer, who entered the octagon with red, open-fingered sparring gloves on. These gloves have padding that covers the knuckles of the fingers and the back of the hand but leaves all the fingers exposed. With all the fingers free and exposed, a fighter can still grab an opponent, which is useful for grappling, but the fighter can still utilize striking techniques. Additionally, the sparring gloves

---

[24] *UFC 2: No Way Out*, (1994; Las Vegas, NV: Zuffa, LLC., 2013), DVD.

[25] *UFC 3: The American Dream*, (1994; Las Vegas, NV: Zuffa, LLC., 2013), DVD.

are lighter than traditional boxing or kickboxing gloves that weigh anywhere from 10- to 16-ounces. These lighter, open-ended gloves are usually worn for pad hitting and pad work that is meant to further a fighter's dexterity, speed, and other abilities. Using them in a fight, though, is innovative. Yet, for some reason, Mitchell took the gloves off prior to the beginning of the bout. No reason was given by the octagon-side announcers, and there were no rules against using this equipment, just as there were no rules against Shamrock wearing his wrestling shoes. In an article on the origins of MMA gloves, writer Lucasz Wieczorek states that referee "Big" John McCarthy asked Mitchell to remove the gloves before the bout started.[26] Indeed, McCarthy is seen walking over to Mitchell and talking with him just before Mitchell removes his gloves. Why McCarthy would do this, though, remains a mystery as the UFC regulations at the time allowed fighters to wear gloves if they chose. Whatever the reason may have been for their removal, it remains that Mitchell was the first to wear such attire into the octagon, albeit briefly.

Fighters continued to innovate, and fight costumes continued to evolve as UFC events continued to be held. UFC 4: Revenge of the Warriors took place on 16 December 1994 and continued the established format of a single elimination round, grand prix style tournament. As before, eight fighters arrived in Tulsa, Oklahoma for the event along with two alternates. A trend was developing where exciting fighters or winners in prior UFCs made returns in other UFCs. An alternate in Tulsa, Kevin Rosier, was an exciting fighter in UFC 1, Royce had been the champion of UFCs 1 and 2, Steve Jennum was the champion of UFC 3, and Keith Hackney was an exciting fighter from UFC 3. All returned for UFC 4. The remaining openings were filled by new, unknown, and untested combatants.

Perhaps it is the better quality in the recording, or perhaps it is the actual usage, but there is a noticeable increase in fighters taking advantage of both groin protection and mouthguards at UFC 4. Furthermore, more fighters are wearing shoes than before, with at least three entering the octagon wearing a pair of boxing or wrestling shoes, whereas only Shamrock wore shoes in UFC 3. Along with this, boxer Melton Bowen wears open-ended sparring gloves into the octagon for his fight against Steve Jennum. Although Bowen loses the fight, the advantage of wearing such gloves is obvious as the octagon-side announcers

---

[26] Lukasz Wieczorek, "Bet you didn't know that! The story behind the MMA gloves," *Martial Arts Unleashed*, October 17, 2019, Accessed February 14, 2023, https://medium.com/martial-arts-unleashed/bet-you-didnt-know-that-the-story-behind-the-mma-gloves-8a563fc0fd01.

discuss how contestants are injuring their hands when striking their opponents. Because of an injury, some have been forced to withdraw from the championship, which deprives them of the opportunity to earn the coveted grand prize payout and the title of UFC champion. This happened to Hackney in UFC 3, who had to withdraw after injuring his hand. Also, fewer fighters than ever are wearing fight costumes traditionally associated with their martial art at UFC 4.

Of course, Royce Gracie entered the octagon for UFC 4 wearing his traditional fight costume. Also, it is true that grapplers like Dan "The Best" Severn are wearing spandex briefs similar to those worn in the WWF, yet Severn and most other grapplers did not participate in the WWF until after their UFC careers ended, if at all. Instead, Severn was a renowned high and collegiate grappler who, according to his own biography, was a two-time national champion in high school and set multiple national records in college before becoming an alternate for the 1984 U.S. Olympic Team.[27] All of this not only illustrates the skill with which Severn fought but also that he should have entered the octagon in a wrestling singlet and wrestling shoes, the same fight costume he wore during his high school and college matches, not the spandex briefs and wrestling shoes he ultimately fought in. Therefore, Severn and others like him chose to wear spandex briefs and wrestling shoes, or just spandex briefs, because they found some benefit in doing so.

The likely benefit is that the combatant has the least amount of clothes on as possible. As the people wearing this fight costume are grapplers, many of whom have a traditional grappling background in high school and college wrestling, they are familiar with how taxing these fights are on the body. They know their bodies will likely produce a lot of sweat, and they know they will become quite fatigued. This will all be exacerbated the more clothing they have on, which is to say they will experience fatigue more quickly and they will produce more sweat. In order to lessen the effects of the martial combat, the grapplers are wearing as little clothing as possible. Another benefit to this fight costume is the sweat that is produced becomes a lubricant that can help the grappler escape the holds of their opponent, or they can advance their martial position in order to gain the advantage. Those with lengthy experience in grappling will know all this as they will have experienced this while working on developing their skills and abilities in the gym throughout their careers as wrestlers. Thus,

---

[27] "About Dan 'The Beast' Severn," Official Site of Dan –The Beast– Severn, Accessed August 31, 2023, http://dansevern.com/about/.

spandex briefs can be advantageous to a fighter like Severn, who has the training and experience to know how to use this fight costume properly in his fight strategy.

In all, then, it seems the fighters are making decisions prior to the contest about fight costumes that they feel will give them the most advantage over their opponent, whomever that may be. Knowing that there are no weight classes and that they can face a person of any size, skill, or ability, those who are about to enter the octagon are doing all they can to ensure they achieve victory in each bout and in the grand prix. For example, tae kwon do practitioner Joe Son wore red wrestling briefs, knee wraps, and wrestling shoes for his match against karate expert Keith Hackney. Hackney wore sweatpants and a tank top, and had his ankles taped for support. Royce has consistently worn his *gi*, but it is obvious in UFC 4 that he is also wearing a mouthguard and groin protection. Yet, Royce's *gi* is an asset in his matches as he can use it to achieve different submission holds on his opponents. Therefore, Royce is doing what the other fighters are doing in that he is dressing for success.

Fighters were not the only people who could, or would, have an effect on their fightwear, though. For these events to continue, they had to make money for the promotors and the financial backers. Therefore, the audience who had watched UFC 1 had to want to watch an as yet unplanned UFC 2, UFC 3, and so on. It is difficult to ascertain audience members' reactions to the first few UFC events directly, as it does not seem that those in attendance were interviewed by the media or anyone else. According to Shamrock, though, some audience members were supposed to come to the UFC 1 after party, but none did, and neither did any invited reporters.[28] Yet, it can be safely concluded that fans were created at UFC 1, and they did not bemoan the results of the athlete's fightwear choices.

It is safe to conclude this as attendance at the events grew, and PPV buys increased with each UFC card for some time. UFC 1 had about 3,000 ticket sales, but because of the limited seating due to the sizes of the different venues, ticket sales remained about the same.[29] The largest difference showed in PPV

---

[28] "Ken Shamrock - UFC 1 20th Anniversary interview part 2/2," Sherdog.com, Evolve Media, January 9, 2017, https://www.youtube.com/watch?v=Rleu6YudsHg&list=PLo0hPpEUaQtD7bkJprbpu5Yed0rDs5oge&index=32&ab_channel=Sherdog.com.

[29] Davie, *Is this Legal?*, 260; Erich Krauss and Bret Aita, *Brawl: A Behind-the-Scenes Look at Mixed Martial Arts Competition* (Toronto: ECW Press, 2002), 16, https://www.hoopladigital.com/play/13630166.

sales, though, with 86,592 for UFC 1 and nearly 120,000 coming in at UFC 2.[30] However, according to *Forbes* magazine, UFC 5 had more than 250,000 buys at $19.95 per purchase in 1995 dollars, equaling roughly $4,987,500 in revenue for SEG from PPV alone.[31] Ticket sales for the arena, international rights, and videocassette sales brought in more revenue for SEG for each of these UFC events. From these figures, it is obvious that both fans and the promotion were happy with the choices the fighters were making regarding their fight costumes and protective gear. This point is supported by the fact that there were no rules made concerning fight costumes for some time. Indeed, as the UFC continued to grow in popularity with each new event, fighters were encouraged to wear what they wanted to so long as the fight was entertaining. Since combatants wanted to win by any means possible and since the rules were scant on how fighters could win a fight (no biting and no eye gouging starting with UFC 2: No Way Out), the fights were usually exciting for the audience. Therefore, it can be concluded that the evolution of fight costumes in the early events of the UFC was directly affected by fighters', audience members', and promoters' desires, although everyone was trying to achieve their desires in their own ways.

Yet, the concerns of another group were starting to affect the UFC as the sport began to grow in popularity. Sports commissioners and politicians were not as excited about the UFC, the fighters, and their fights as the fans and the promotion. Whereas fans enjoyed the bouts and flocked to the arenas or paid increasing sums for the live pay-per-view experience, politicians and commissioners went the opposite route. Rather, they became vocal about the violence of the UFC bouts after reading newspaper articles in such publications as The New York Times or the Los Angeles Times or elsewhere. Many articles did not provide a positive assessment of any UFC event. For example, Richard Sandomir writes about the upcoming UFC 2 for The New York Times on 8 March 1994, saying, "Clearly, there's a bloodthirsty sucker born every minute."[32] Another article published on 7 September 1994 in the Globe & Mail in Toronto, Canada, reads, "The spectacle has been compared to cockfighting in human form, and features experts in martial arts – from karate to kung

---

[30] Davie, *Is this Legal?.* Thousands Get Kicks from 'Reality Combat,'" *Chicago Tribune,* August 31, 1994, Proquest One Academic.

[31] Randall Lane, "It's Live, It's Brutal," *Forbes,* May 22, 1995, 48.

[32] Richard Sandomir, "TV SPORTS; Death Is Cheap: Maybe It's Just $14.95," *The New York Times,* March 8, 1994, Gale In Context: Biography.

fu…The winner is whoever is left standing in the ring…"[33] These articles were somewhat dramatic in the language used as not all the fights were bloody bouts, and many combatants in the first several UFC contests included experienced martial artists or those who claimed to be so. Additionally, the bouts usually ended pretty quickly and without any gore. The short bouts and lack of violence occasionally led to problems for SEG, who had to find ways to fill time and keep those in attendance entertained. None of this is a defense of the UFC or the fights, but it does demonstrate that the authors of many of the articles of the first several UFCs were convinced the new sport was a bloodsport.

Commissioners and politicians who watched the events or read the previously mentioned and other newspaper articles started moving to outlaw MMA events in their states. UFC 2: No Way Out was moved from its initial venue to the Mammoth Gardens Event Center because the mayor of Denver had canceled the lease on the original venue in an attempt to stop the event.[34] Then, after UFC: The Ultimate Ultimate, held on 16 December 1995, Mayor Wellington Webb of Denver stated there would be no further events within the city limits.[35] At the same time, nearly twenty states were considering banning the events outright. Senator John McCain of Arizona, after finding out about UFC 4, is reported to have said it was "vicious and bloody" and then worked to have the PPV canceled.[36]

When UFC 8: David and Goliath was scheduled to be held in Puerto Rico on 16 February 1996, politicians from Washington D.C. decided to take SEG to federal court in an attempt to have the event stopped. So, just before UFC 8, John McCarthy, a Los Angeles Police Department officer, Gracie jiu-jitsu devotee, and UFC referee, was in federal court arguing to have the event allowed. The negative impact MMA was having on boxing events revenue and advertising revenue may have been a reason to have MMA banned in every state in the U.S.[37] It is true that many politicians around the country supported

---

[33] Gale in Context: Opposing Viewpoints. "Middle Kingdom Human Rites: How TV turns back the clock," *Globe & Mail*, September 7, 1994, p. A14.

[34] Krauss and Aita, *Brawl*, 16, https://www.hoopladigital.com/play/13630166.

[35] Andrea Stone, "Bare-knuckle debate//Fans see fun in brawls where anything goes," *USA Today* (McLean, VA), December 18, 1995.

[36] Oscar Dixon, "Holding Court," *USA Today* (McLean, VA), December 15, 1994, 01C, ProQuest One Academic.

[37] Rogan and McCarthy, "JRE MMA Show #26 with Big John McCarthy."

boxing as a legitimate sporting event but saw the burgeoning sport of MMA as "human cockfighting." Senator McCain, who boxed while at the naval academy and was a lifelong advocate of the sport, was a key witness in court calling for the end of the UFC in every state.

Arguments were made in court by both those in favor of the sport of MMA and arguments against the sport of MMA. The arguments centered around the violence of MMA versus the violence of other combat sports, such as wrestling or boxing, with an expert on the sport of boxing testifying on how boxing gloves make the sport safer for the athletes who are receiving repeated punches to the body and head. McCarthy countered this argument, demonstrating that the gloves primarily protect the hands of the boxer throwing the punches. However, the body or head of the fighter receiving the punches from the gloved hand is still being seriously damaged. In short, McCarthy argued that if the safety of fighters is truly the concern of the regulators and politicians, those fighting with ungloved hands are fighting more safely than those fighting with protected, gloved hands because those who are protecting their hands are less concerned with injuring themselves. Jimmerson, the boxer who fought in UFC 1, confirmed this point in an interview marking the twentieth anniversary of that event, saying that boxers get their hands wrapped up past the first knuckles for additional cushioning and support, as this provides further protection from injury when landing punches.[38] These arguments, then, showed that the UFC had fighters who were more concerned with protecting their hands by avoiding strikes to the head. Thus, this made the UFC a safer sport than boxing. However, in 1996, regulators, politicians, and traditionalists did not agree with McCarthy or Jimmerson.[39]

The result of these attacks on the sport of MMA in general and the UFC promotion in particular nearly ended both. Revenue declined sharply for the UFC as it became difficult to televise its events on pay-per-view because of the negative publicity. Also, due to the negative stigma related to the sport and the promotion, multiple states passed legislation banning the contests entirely. All of this forced the UFC into smaller venues that further reduced its ticket sales. Additionally, instead of receiving revenue from PPV sales, SEG soon only received revenue from video sales both within the United States and overseas. Sales within the U.S., though, were difficult to come by as outlets were loathe

[38] "Art Jimmerson - UCF 1 20th Anniversary Memories part 2/2," Sherdog.com, Evolve Media, January 8, 2017, https://www.youtube.com/watch?v=dHlgYi-s8h8&list=PLo0hPpEUaQtD7bkJprbpu5Yed0rDs5oge&index=38&ab_channel=Sherdog.com.
[39] Rogan and McCarthy, "JRE MMA Show #26 with Big John McCarthy."

to sell or rent recordings of UFC events. However, people still wanted to attend the contests or watch them from the luxury of their homes. Despite their best efforts, politicians and the commissioners of regulating bodies could not stop the UFC juggernaut.

By late 1996, the once mighty UFC and its controlling financial interest, SEG, were looking at an uncertain future. Everything that had already occurred, though, could not be undone. Early in the history of the UFC, fighters could wear whatever they deemed suitable for the combat they were about to undertake. It is important to note that by UFC 6: Clash of Titans, which took place on 14 July 1995, fight costumes associated with a particular martial art had largely been abandoned. Therefore, at UFC 6, when Rudyard Moncayo, a kenpo karate blackbelt, fought Pat Smith, a kickboxer who had fought earlier in UFCs 1 and 2 wearing Muay Thai boxing shorts, neither entered the combat area in traditional fightwear. Rather, Moncayo wore black, form-fitting spandex compression pants, whereas Smith wore a white wrestling singlet. Going forward to UFC 10: The Tournament, which was held on 12 July 1996, nearly all the fighters were wearing either spandex briefs, compression shorts or pants, or athletic shorts into the octagon, with some occasional exceptions.

Furthermore, fighters could wear gloves from the start of the UFC if they wanted to, and one fighter chose to wear one glove in UFC 1. After this, gloves were largely abandoned by all fighters for nearly three years. In fact, wrestling or boxing shoes were worn more often than any type of gloves for the first nine UFCs. It has already been noted that Felix Lee Mitchell was the first to wear fingerless gloves into the octagon at UFC 3, but he took them off just before the bout started. Melton Bowen wore the same type of gloves for the duration of his bout at UFC 4, but lost to Steve Jennum. D. L. "Tank" Abbott always wore fingerless gloves for his fights, starting with his debut at UFC 6, but he is the exception that proves the rule. It is interesting to note the reason Abbott wore his fingerless gloves from the outset of his career, though. According to a recent article by Case Harts of *Bloody Elbow*, Abbott wore gloves to protect his hands as he was fond of brawling, or fighting without restraint or strategy, when he got in the octagon despite the fact that he had decades of grappling experience by the time he started his UFC career.[40] This reason aligns with what McCarthy said in court in 1996 and what Jimmerson would say later.

---

[40] Case Harts, "Why do MMA Fighters Wear Gloves," *Bloody Elbow*, July 20, 2023, https://bloodyelbow.com/2023/07/20/why-do-mma-fighters-wear-gloves/.

Gloves started to become more standard fightwear at UFC 9: Motor City Madness, which was on May 17, 1996. However, it was at UFC 10 where half of all the contestants wore fingerless gloves. This was a marked step forward in the transition of the UFC and MMA fight costume as it demonstrated the utility of this particular piece of equipment. Fighters experienced the advantage of protecting their hands against injury while striking and also knew they could still grapple with their opponent if the fight made its way to the ground. Fighters making the personal choice to protect their hands is further support for what McCarthy said in court before UFC 8. Gloves would continue to be a choice for fighters until UFC 14: Showdown, which took place on 27 July 1997. In addition to this, starting with UFC 4, mouthguards and groin protection became more prevalent, but it was still a fighter's choice to wear gloves, mouthguards, or groin protection. As there were no regulations regarding any fighting equipment or fight costumes, UFC contestants made all these choices individually because they wanted to win their fights as well as win the cash prize, the esteem of their peers, and the glory of being a UFC champion. Starting with UFC 14, though, gloves became mandatory fightwear for all fighters who entered the octagon as MMA was increasingly becoming a nationally regulated sport rather than a regionally regulated sport.[41] Mouthguards and groin protection also became mandatory at UFC 14.

Along with making gloves mandatory, the parent company of the UFC, Semaphore Entertainment Group, initiated the change to shorts rather than allowing fighters to wear whatever they chose to when they entered the octagon. This was an attempt to get the UFC sanctioned in more states so that the sport could be televised nationwide and have its events in arenas throughout the nation. To further these ends, SEG also discontinued the use of footwear and eagerly sought out a standardized set of rules, which would ultimately become the Unified Rules of Mixed Martial Arts. However, before any of this could happen, SEG ended up selling the UFC.

Zuffa, who bought the UFC from SEG in January 2001, would continue to seek standardized rules and fight costumes, as well as regulation from various regulatory bodies.[42] Both companies did all of this in an attempt to increase the marketability and profitability of the UFC; in short, the promotors wanted

---

[41] Wieczorek, "Bet you didn't know that! The story behind the MMA gloves."

[42] Adam Hill, "A Timeline of UFC Rules: From No-Holds-Barred to Highly Regulated," *Bleacher Report*, April 24, 2013, accessed February 14, 2023, https://bleacherreport.com/articles/1614213-a-timeline-of-ufc-rules-from-no-holds-barred-to-highly-regulated.

more money, so they eagerly and actively sought to increase the appeal of their product through self-imposed regulation. The incentives to regulate the product and increase its appeal are what ultimately did away with the earlier form of the UFC fightwear, which was whatever the fighter wished to wear for the fight. By the time SEG sold the rights to the UFC to Zuffa, shorts, fight gloves, mouthguards, and groin protection were already standard fightwear required for every fighter to wear before entering the octagon. The same year Zuffa bought the UFC, the Unified Rules of Mixed Martial Arts began to be accepted by state athletic commissions across the country. The Association of Boxing Commissions, a North American boxing and mixed martial arts governing body that operates in the United States and Canada, would accept these rules in 2009.[43] What would change when Zuffa took over the UFC would be the appearance of the gloves and shorts as well as who made this fightwear.

Fightwear in the UFC has continued to change for over 20 years now since Zuffa, Inc., then Endeavor Group Holdings, bought the promotion. Dana White, the CEO of the organization for the last two decades, has made it part of his business plan to sign contracts with new product makers and distributers so as to further the industry and brand saturation of the UFC. The most recent UFC fightwear product maker for fighter shorts and tops is Venum, but before them was Reebok, and before Reebok, it was TapouT. There was a point there when TapouT was the official clothing of the UFC, but fighters could have their own sponsors and apparel as well. It is worth noting the two divergent branches in the evolution of UFC fight costumes that occurred after Zuffa, Inc., purchased the promotion. The one branch involves the contract with TapouT as the official fightwear of the UFC. This is an important step in White's overall business strategy as he and Zuffa, Inc. looked to make the UFC a household name and MMA a legitimate sport. The second branch in the evolution of fight costumes that fighters could and did develop their own fight apparel and brands in order to increase their revenue stream.

As already stated, the UFC under SEG and then under Zuffa, Inc. worked diligently to standardize fight costumes and fight equipment. Under Zuffa, this came to fruition when TapouT became the official sponsor of UFC Ultimate Fighter 7, which premiered on 2 April 2008. This sponsorship allowed TapouT exclusive apparel integration in all 12 episodes of the season, according to *MMA News* at the time, and it allowed TapouT to air exclusive commercials on

---

[43] Hill, *Bleacher Report*, 12-15.

the Spike TV network.[44] This agreement is somewhat similar to Nike's current deal with the National Football League in that Nike has exclusive rights to provide all the players of the NFL their team's uniforms and can air exclusive game day commercials on NFL Network. However, the deal with TapouT was finalized in 2008, long after the premier of the UFC in 1993 and the first ten UFC events that this study is focused on. In fact, the contract with TapouT was signed nearly seven years after Zuffa, Inc. purchased the UFC from SEG in 2001. So, fighters were able to wear their own fight costumes made by whomever and bought with whatever funds they had so long as they met the requirements of the Unified Rules of Mixed Martial Arts. The Unified Rules allowed for Muay Thai shorts, spandex briefs, and board shorts.

The second branch in the evolution of fight costumes in the UFC involves fighters developing their own fightwear, clothing, and brands. Yet, this topic is somewhat beyond the scope of the current study, so it will not be discussed in detail. Generally, though, since the earliest fights in the UFC, fighters could and did wear whatever they felt would give them the advantage. TapouT quickly emerged as a favorite of UFC athletes after it was created in 1997. As fighters began to earn money in the octagon, they invested their funds in different ventures, sought out sponsorship deals, or both, in order to increase their financial advantage. Investing in clothing brand startups seemed like a good strategy, as fighters could wear their apparel on their pre-fight walks to the octagon, and fans would see this. The fighters could also wear their apparel on media days, fan meet-and-greets, post-fight interviews, and basically any time they might be out-and-about in order to get the brand as much attention as possible. Doing so might increase sales of the athlete's personal apparel and thus increase their revenue stream. In addition to all this, fighters were able to have sponsors buy spots on their fightwear in much the same way NASCAR drivers have decals of their sponsors on their cars. For example, fighters could sell a spot on their shorts to a sponsor, thus earning revenue for the ad space. Therefore, fighters wore fightwear, usually some sort of shorts, to the octagon with sponsors' logos in several different spots. There also might be sponsor information on the fighter's t-shirt that would be seen in the post-fight interview.

So far, men have been the focus of the discussion as they were the only individuals fighting in the UFC and other major promotions since the outset.

---

[44] Michael Shalik, "TapouT Named Official Sponsor For The Ultimate Fighter 7," March 13, 2008, *MMA News*, https://www.mmanews.com/news/tapout-named-official-sponsor-for-the-ultimate-fighter-7.

However, the first fight involving female combatants in the UFC took place on 23 February 2013.[45] This fight was between Ronda Rousey and Liz Carmouche, both of whom came into the UFC at a time when fighters could still take advantage of personalizing their apparel and seeking out their own sponsors. Just like the men, these possibilities increased the revenue potential for female athletes. The fightwear and protective equipment for females was and continues to be different in some respects, though. Although TapouT was the official brand of the UFC at the time, as already stated, athletes could wear what they liked as long as Unified Rules were met. Women did and do wear Muay Thai shorts, spandex briefs, and board shorts like their male counterparts, but their shorts tend to be shorter in length and more form fitting than the male shorts. This is to say that the spandex briefs are shorter than those worn by males, the Muay Thai shorts, which are short in length for both genders, are shorter for women, and the board shorts are also shorter in length than those worn by males. This is likely purposefully done by apparel designers as females have a sex appeal for a largely male audience that males simply do not have. Female fighters could choose to wear looser fitting shorts, yet many did not. Like the males, females understood the advantages and disadvantages of their fightwear and protective equipment. For example, looser fitting shorts can become cumbersome and heavy as the fight progresses, and they are sodden with sweat.

Though women wore shorts like the males, they wore tops, unlike the male fighters. According to the Unified Rules, male fighters must fight in shorts or spandex briefs only unless they are utilizing some sort of protective equipment such as ankle or knee wraps. Women can use these, too, but women wear tight fitting t-shirts that are similar to sweat-wicking Under Armor shirts seen on many athletes today, or they wear a tight-fitting spandex sports bra. This fightwear is instrumental for many reasons, not the least of which is the comfort of the female athletes while engaging in combat, but also for the comfort of the audience in attendance and watching on TV. MMA fights in the UFC are intended to simulate street fights or fights between two masters of different disciplines that take place in a location where almost anything can happen. Yet, these are regulated fights that have rules intended to limit some of

---

[45] Marc Raimondi, "MMA anniversary: How Ronda Rousey vs. Liz Carmouche impacted Amanda Nunes and other stars," February 23, 2021, *ESPN*, https://www.espn.com/mma/story/_/id/28239468/mma-anniversary-how-ronda-rousey-vs-liz-carmouche-impacted-amanda-nunes-other-stars.

what might happen, such as punches to the groin, eye gouging, and, once women came to the UFC, the intended or unintended exposing of breasts. Furthermore, these tops are worn tightly to suppress or hold down the breasts in order to keep them from becoming more damaged than necessary during a fight.

With the change to exclusive brands, though, all this ended. As already mentioned, TapouT became the official sponsor of UFC's Ultimate Fighter 7 in 2008, and then it became the official lifestyle apparel brand in 2012.[46] Then, Reebok took over this role as the UFC's exclusive clothing outfitter in 2015, but the deal started with disappointment. The apparel worn by fighters in the octagon and what was available to fans outside it left much to be desired, especially after fans and fighters had such a great experience with the TapouT brand. The change was made from Reebok to Venum because many fans and White were outspoken about the look of the Reebok fightwear shorts and tops; this is to say, neither fans nor White liked the appearance of the Reebok apparel. So, when the contract was up for reconsideration, White looked elsewhere, and Venum won the bid to supply the UFC with fighter apparel. Thus, Venum apparel became the new UFC exclusive outfitter in 2021. So far, the reaction to the new apparel has been positive. Venum also supplies fighters with their shorts and tops for ONE Championship fights and Bellator MMA fights, so this is a company that has worldwide experience in providing appealing, eye-catching fighter performance apparel that people will recognize from the United States to China to Australia and many places in between.

The overall impact of these brand deals on general sports retail is hard to determine. The UFC deals with TapouT, Reebok, and Venum all seemed to model apparel deals that had already taken place in other sports. According to Sports Illustrated writer Tim Layden, the NFL Properties was formed in 1963, with the other leagues following suite.[47] The purpose of these property organizations was to collect royalties on merchandise, but there were regulations or stipulations until much later. In fact, it was not until the early 2000s that the NBA and NFL required a single apparel brand to make all the

---

[46] Michael Long, "UFC names Tapout as its official lifestyle apparel brand," February 7, 2012, *SportsPro*, https://www.sportspromedia.com/news/ufc_names_tapout_as_its_official_lifestyle_apparel_brand/?zephr_sso_ott=YxfBJH.

[47] Tim Layden, "We are what we wear: How sports jerseys became ubiquitous in the U.S.," February 1, 2016, *Sports Illustrated*, https://www.si.com/nfl/2016/02/01/mlb-nba-nhl-sports-jersys-rise-popularity.

teams' uniforms.[48] It can be seen from these sources, then, that the UFC was modeling its business strategy regarding fighter apparel on that of other sports organizations. Their strategy ultimately paid off with the signing of Venum to a long-term contract deal. As other sports leagues have changed their apparel producers, the UFC might try a different brand in the future as well, such as Nike or some other designer. Yet, standardization of fight costumes and fighter equipment is the motivation behind any changes the UFC might make.

Along with the standardization of fight costumes in the UFC and other promotions, MMA gloves have been standardized around the world in major promotions at a four-ounce weight per glove. They also share the features of covering the back of the hand and the knuckles, or the head of the metacarpals, while wrapping around the balls of the hand but keeping the palm of the hand largely free of material. Furthermore, there is material extending along the proximal portion of each finger, essentially covering the first part of the finger that comes out from the knuckle of the hand to the first knuckle of each finger. Gloves are made of leather and come in whatever color the promotion wishes. For the UFC and ONE Championship, the gloves are black with promotion logos on them. However, for Bellator MMA, the gloves are all red for the fighter from the red corner and all blue for the fighter from the blue corner, except in the World Grand Prix championship fights, where the gloves are all white for both corners.

For the UFC, though, the process to get to standardized fightwear was long and arduous. Courts, regulators, politicians, fighters, promoters, and fans were all involved to varying degrees. Overall, the main goal of any fighting apparel or gear worn in a ring or cage is to protect a fighter while also providing enough martial action to keep the audience interested and coming back for more. The UFC and other promotions are continually trying to achieve a perfect balance that will keep fans interested in what is occurring in the fighting area while also holding regulators at bay. The fighter, meanwhile, just wants to fight and to win by any means possible.

Bibliography

"About Dan 'The Beast' Severn." Official Site of Dan –The Beast– Severn. Accessed August 31, 2023. http://dansevern.com/about/.

---

[48] "NFL Jersey Licenses Timeline. A rich history Starter, Reebok, Nike Adidas and more," August 12, 2020, *Wolfgang Sport*, Accessed August 31, 2023, https://www.wolfgangsport.com/nfl-jersey-licenses-timeline/.

"About One." One Championship. Accessed February 10, 2023. https://www.onefc.com/about-us/.

"Art Jimmerson - UCF 1 20th Anniversary Memories part 2/2." Sherdog.com. Evolve Media. January 8, 2017. https://www.youtube.com/watch?v=dHlgYi-s8h8&list=PLo0hPpEUaQtD7bkJprbpu5Yed0rDs5oge&index=38&ab_channel=Sherdog.com.

Davie, Art. *Is this Legal? The Inside Story of the First UFC From The Man Who Created It,* with Sean Wheelock. Olathe, KS: Ascend Books, 2014.

Di Marino, Stefano. *A Complete Guide to Kickboxing.* New York: Enslow Publishing, LLC., 2018. https://www.hoopladigital.com/play/12172211.

Dixon, Oscar. "Holding Court," *USA Today* (McLean, VA), December 15, 1994, 01C, ProQuest One Academic.

Gale in Context: Opposing Viewpoints. "Middle Kingdom Human Rites: How TV turns back the clock," *Globe & Mail,* September 7, 1994.

"Grand Master Carlos Gracie: The Beginning of Everything." Rilion Gracie Jiu-Jitsu. Accessed December 30, 2021. https://www.riliongracie.com/carlos-gracie/.

Harts, Case. "Why do MMA Fighters Wear Gloves," *Bloody Elbow.* July 20, 2023, https://bloodyelbow.com/2023/07/20/why-do-mma-fighters-wear-gloves/.

Hill, Adam. "A Timeline of UFC Rules: From No-Holds-Barred to Highly Regulated," *Bleacher Report.* April 24, 2013. Accessed February 14, 2023, https://bleacherreport.com/articles/1614213-a-timeline-of-ufc-rules-from-no-holds-barred-to-highly-regulated.

Hisataka, Masayuki Kukan. *Scientific Karatedo.* Rutland, VT: Charles E. Tuttle Company, 1996. https://www.hoopladigital.com/play/11784540.

"ie lavalava "PUMA" (cloth wrap around)." Accessed January 5, 2022. Cotton cloth, 1115mm (height), 1750mm (length). Museum of New Zealand. https://collections.tepapa.govt.nz/object/1151647.

Juul, Matt. "Dennis Hallman's Shorts: Dana White Speaks About Speedo & More." *Bleacher Report.* August 8, 2011. https://bleacherreport.com/articles/796989-ufc-133-hallman-speaks-out-about-speedo-arm-injury.

"Ken Shamrock - UFC 1 20th Anniversary interview part 1/2." Sherdog.com. Evolve Media. January 9, 2017. https://www.youtube.com/watch?v=A1qytQBtxgk&list=PLo0hPpEUaQtD7bkJprbpu5Yed0rDs5oge&index=31&ab_channel=Sherdog.com.

"Ken Shamrock - UFC 1 20th Anniversary interview part 2/2." Sherdog.com. Evolve Media. January 9, 2017. https://www.youtube.com/watch?v=Rleu6YudsHg&list=PLo0hPpEUaQtD7bkJprbpu5Yed0rDs5oge&index=32&ab_channel=Sherdog.com.

Kriegel, Mark. "Jim Brown is shilling for sick thrills," *The Evening Sun,* March 8, 1994, 8C.

Krauss, Erich and Bret Aita. *Brawl: A Behind-the-Scenes Look at Mixed Martial Arts Competition.* Toronto: ECW Press, 2002. https://www.hoopladigital.com/play/13630166.

Lane, Randall. "It's Live, It's Brutal." *Forbes.* May 22, 1995.

Layden, Tim. "We are what we wear: How sports jerseys became ubiquitous in the U.S." February 1, 2016. *Sports Illustrated.* https://www.si.com/nfl/2016/02/01/mlb-nba-nhl-sports-jersys-rise-popularity.

Long, Michael. "UFC names Tapout as its official lifestyle apparel brand." February 7, 2012. *SportsPro.* https://www.sportspromedia.com/news/ufc_names_tapout_as_its_official_lifestyle_apparel_brand/?zephr_sso_ott=YxfBJH.

Lucas, Mark, dir. *UFC 1: The Beginning.* 1993; Las Vegas, NV: Zuffa, LLC., 2013. DVD.

Martelli, Joe. "WWE's Evolution in the 1980's: What the World Is Watching." *Bleacher Report.* April 8, 2010. https://bleacherreport.com/articles/375317-what-the-world-is-watching-wwes-evolution-in-the-1980s.

"NFL Jersey Licenses Timeline. A rich history Starter, Reebok, Nike Adidas and more." August 12, 2020. *Wolfgang Sport.* Accessed August 31, 2023. https://www.wolfgangsport.com/nfl-jersey-licenses-timeline/.

"Pancrase 3: Yes, We Are Hybrid Wrestlers 3." Tapology.com. Accessed February 10, 2023. https://www.tapology.com/fightcenter/events/3651-pancrase-3-yes-we-are-hybrid-wrestlers-3.

Proquest One Academic. "Thousands Get Kicks from Reality Combat," *Chicago Tribune*, August 31, 1994.

Raimondi, Marc. "MMA anniversary: How Ronda Rousey vs. Liz Carmouche impacted Amanda Nunes and other stars." February 23, 2021. *ESPN.* https://www.espn.com/mma/story/_/id/28239468/mma-anniversary-how-ronda-rousey-vs-liz-carmouche-impacted-amanda-nunes-other-stars.

Rogan, Joe and "Big" John McCarthy. "JRE MMA Show #26 with Big John McCarthy." May 15, 2018. *Joe Rogan Experience.* Produced by Jamie Vernon. Podcast, video and MP3 audio, 2:26:12. https://open.spotify.com/episode/277VQ10aGB2fGbOGKnVI6u.

Sandomir, Richard. "TV SPORTS; Death Is Cheap: Maybe It's Just $14.95," *The New York Times*, March 8, 1994, Gale In Context: Biography.

Shalik, Michael. "TapouT Named Official Sponsor For The Ultimate Fighter 7." March 13, 2008. *MMA News.* https://www.mmanews.com/news/tapout-named-official-sponsor-for-the-ultimate-fighter-7.

Stets, Michael. "UFC 1: Story behind Art Jimmerson and the lone boxing glove revealed." MMAMania.com. November 16, 2013. https://www.mmamania.com/2013/11/16/5109964/ufc-1-story-art-jimmerson-lone-boxing-glove-mma.

Stone, Andrea. "Bare-knuckle debate//Fans see fun in brawls where anything goes," *USA Today* (McLean, VA), December 18, 1995.

UFC 3: The American Dream. 1994; Las Vegas, NV: Zuffa, LLC., 2013. DVD.

"UFC founder Rorion Gracie talks early UFC experience (Part 2/2)." Sherdog.com. Evolve Media. December 22, 2016. https://www.youtube.com/watch?v=BOvYRsUD4AQ&ab_channel=Sherdog.com.

UFC 2: No Way Out. 1994; Las Vegas, NV: Zuffa, LLC., 2013. DVD.

Wells, Garrison. *Brazilian Jiu Jitsu: Ground Fighting Combat.* Minneapolis: Lerner Publications Company, 2012. https://www.hoopladigital.com/play/11773517.

"What's PANCRASE?" World Pancrase Create Inc. Accessed February 9, 2023, https://www.pancrase.co.jp/en/htm/wht.html.

Wieczorek, Lukasz. "Bet you didn't know that! The story behind the MMA gloves." *Martial Arts Unleashed.* October 17, 2019. Accessed February 14, 2023. https://medium.com/martial-arts-unleashed/bet-you-didnt-know-that-the-story-behind-the-mma-gloves-8a563fc0fd01.

"Zane Frazier - UFC 1 20th anniversary interview part 1/2." Sherdog.com. Evolve Media. January 9, 2017. https://www.youtube.com/watch?v=nLoWqtboP3o&list=PLo0hPpEUaQtD7bkJprbpu5Yed0rDs5oge&index=36&ab_channel=Sherdog.com.

Further Reading

"MMA Uniform History." *Epic Sports.* Accessed November 27, 2021. https://mma.epicsports.com/mma-uniform-history.html.

Overtime Heroics Editorial. "The Story Of The UFC-Reebok Deal, And Fight Gear Through The Ages." October 24, 2021. *Overtime Heroics.* Accessed August 31, 2023. https://www.overtimeheroics.net/2021/10/24/the-story-of-the-ufc-reebok-deal/.

Chapter 3

Attire and Narrative in Virgil's *Aeneid*

Linda Florence Matheson
University of California at Davis

Abstract: The Aeneid inspires both sight and insight in large part by its use of material culture, often in the form of items of dress. The study examines select narratives constructed around vestments, and discusses how Virgil directs micro-level, personal clothing items to probe and question macrolevel themes such as the cost of war and empire-building. Using modern western social theory, it tracks dress as it carries and transmits culturally ascribed messages that expand metaphysical and historical meaning in this early cannon of literature where clothing items act as devices to shape and construct the narrative, mold character, and advance the plot. This study considers how clothing images embedded within this ancient volume function to convey the cultural convictions of the civilizations from which the text arises.

Keywords: Attire, Virgil's Aeneid, Antiquity, Material culture, Vestments, Dyes, Toga, Embroidery, Aeneas, Dido

***

This work examines the contribution of dress to the narrative process in Virgil's Aeneid, the epic that commemorates Rome, destined to rule the world with the first emperor, Augustus Caesar. Hailed as canonical while still being written and celebrated by the Emperor in 17 BCE as a masterpiece of poetry and patriotism, the Aeneid was swiftly adopted as both "school text and part of the furniture of the mind for educated Romans." According to T. S. Eliot, it has exerted a major influence on art, literature, and politics in Europe for the last 1,800 years.[1] This

---

[1] Charles Martindale, "Introduction: 'The Classic of all Europe,'" (1-18) in *The Cambridge Companion to Virgil* ed. Charles Martindale (Cambridge: Cambridge UP, 1997), 1. Martindale references T.S. Eliot in the first page of this book.

chapter discusses specific passages in which Virgil, whose full name is Publius Vergilius Maro (71-21 BCE), uses micro-level dress items to question macro-level themes like the cost of war, patriarchy, and empire building. Employing modern Western social theory, it tracks these items as they carry and transmit culturally ascribed messages that expand historical meaning. The dress items act as devices that construct, shape, and propel the plot, character, and narrative, because they convey cultural convictions and ambiguities of the civilization from which the text arises.[2]

The significance of dress is often attributed to the emergence of nation-states and capitalist markets in Europe from the fourteenth century onwards, when some scholars acknowledged articles of dress as totems and signs signifying social, economic, or religious identity. Yet, this examination reveals that although dress maintains importance today, the significance of modern capitalism with its commodity culture in ascribing its importance may be exaggerated.[3] A close look at dress in the Aeneid demonstrates how central it is to the ancient world in revealing, transforming, and sustaining social, political, and moral hierarchies, and as a narrative tool in its literature.

The narrative use of dress in the ancient cannons has already been the subject of some stimulating investigations, and I extend my deepest gratitude to the scholars who have preceded me in producing them.[4] Yet, despite the research

---

[2] Parts of this essay have been reworked from "Virgil's Aeneid," chapter four of my dissertation, *Divinely Attired*, University of California, Davis, 2012.

[3] Scholars such as Herbert Spencer, "Badges and Costumes," in *The Principles of Sociology*, (New York: Appleton, 1924); Emile Durkheim, *The Elementary Forms of Religious Life*, Trans. Carol Cosman, (New York: Oxford UP, 2001); Georg Simmel, "Fashion." *International Quarterly* 10:1(1990): 130-155; Karl Marx, *The Social and Political Thought of Karl Marx*, (Cambridge: UP, 1970); Mary Douglas, and Baron Isherwood, *The World of Goods: Toward and Anthropology of Consumption* (New York: Basic, 1979) and others too numerous to list have advanced this theory.

[4] These scholars include Giovanni Fanfani, Mary Harlow, and Mary Louise Nosch, eds., *Spinning Fates and The Song of the Loom: The Use of Textiles, Clothing and Cloth Production as Metaphor, Symbol and Narrative Device in Greek and Latin Literature*, Textile History, (Oxford: Oxbow Books 2016); Mary Harlow, *Literary Representations, in M. Harlow (ed.), A Cultural History of Dress and Fashion*, vol. 1 *Antiquity*, (London: Bloomsbury Academic, 2016); Jane Snyder, "The Web of Song: Weaving Imagery in Homer and the Lyric Poets," *The Classical Journal* 76:3 (1981): 192-198; Henry Bender, "De Habitu Vestis: Clothing in the Aeneid," in *The World of Roman Costume*, (146-152); Mary Vogelzang and W. J. van Bekkum. "Meaning and Symbolism of Clothing in Ancient Near Eastern Texts," in *Scripta Signa Vocis*. ed. H. L. J. Vanstiphout, (Groningren: E. Forsten,

accomplished, more is needed. My hope is that this contribution inspires additional forays into the fascinating employment of dress in ancient world literature.

Forwarding this fascinating employment is Virgil, whom scholars agree excels as one of the last writers in antiquity who successfully cultivates the visual.[5] Especially important is his use of material culture, particularly items of dress, to display and convey culturally complex messages, which by their very nature resist direct explication, yet signify the assumptions and prejudices of Virgil's Rome. In this role as provocateur, these items supply visual ideas that reflect both popular culture and contemporary ideology. By examining select passages that hinge on these vestimentary vehicles, I demonstrate how Virgil links dress to prominent ideological, political, and mythological themes of Roman history, and surreptitiously questions what is going on in Rome at the time he is writing the *Aeneid.*

Equally questioning, although more than nineteen-hundred years later, cultural historian Walter Benjamin's musings on "historical materialism" support this reading of the *Aeneid.* Benjamin's practice of interpreting material culture within historical literature to expand understanding of both epic and era is congruent with Virgil's use of attire. By linking the heightened graphicness of specific dress items to the history of the empire, Virgil enables us to discover the

---

1986), 265-284; Alicia J. Batten, "Clothing and Adornment," *Biblical Theology Bulletin: A Journal of Bible and Theology* 40:3 (2010); 148-159; Jung Hoon Kim, *The Significance of Clothing Imagery,* (London: T and T Clark, 2004). Also deserving my thanks are the following scholars who have contributed greatly to the field of Roman dress in general: Judith Lynn Sebesta and Larissa Bonfante, eds. *The World of Roman Costume,* (Madison, Wis.: UP, 2001); Liza Cleland, Glenys Davis and Lloyd Lewellyn-Jones, eds., *Greek and Roman Dress from A to Z,* (London and New York: Routledge, 2007); Kelly Olsen, *Dress and the Roman Women: Self-Presentation and Society,* (London and New York: Routledge, 2007); and Alexandra T. Croom, *Roman Clothing and Fashion,* (Stroud, Gloucestershire: Tempus, 2002). Others deserve acknowledgement, but space does not allow.

[5] Wendell Clausen, *Virgil's Aeneid: Decorum, Allusion, and Ideology,* (Leipzig: K. G. Saur München, 2002), 12, notes the importance of dress in the *Aeneid,* and how it is described for dramatic effect; W. Ralph Johnson, *Darkness Visible: A Study of Vergil's Aeneid,* (Berkeley: UP, 1976), underscore the importance of the visual; also Philip R. Hardie, *Vergil's Aeneid: Cosmo and Imperium,* (Oxford: UP, 1986) spends time analyzing visual elements of the poem; and Alessandro Barchiesi, "Virgilian Narrative: Ecphrasis," in *The Cambridge Companion,* (Cambridge: Cambridge UP, 1997) 271-282 claims that more than any other ancient poet, Virgil emphasizes the role of the reader in his construction of visual meaning.

themes that dominate the total epic in small micro-level items.[6] Also consistent with this investigation is the work of Roland Barthes, who notes that because dress like literature, "... reflects and inflects people's way of thinking [it] represents a form of historical and sociological mentality."[7] This mentality is valuable in understanding the nuances that narrative dress presents. Also useful is the seminal work on gifting by cultural anthropologist Marcel Mauss, with his research that extends to ancient Rome and beyond.[8] Supplementing the work of these towering minds is that of no lesser scholar, Erving Goffman, on "demeanor" and "deference," which supplies insight into veiling, one of Virgil's physical and psychological uses for written dress.[9]

"Lords of the World": Roman Identity and the Toga

As a vehicle of commemoration of Rome and Emperor Augustus, the *Aeneid* embodies ideals that constitute Roman identity. In its opening book, Jupiter ordains one such ideal when he compares the "toga-bearing Romans" to "Lords of the world" (1.379), demonstrating how the favored garment, the toga, a term derived from the Latin verb "to cover," represents the identity of these masters of the world. [10] Although the toga is being worn when Virgil is writing the epic, and he calls Romans the gens togata - togate race. Aeneas is not yet a Roman, so he does not wear one. Still, the Aeneid increases the toga's importance when Augustus decrees that failure to wear it is worthy of reprimand, thus endorsing the toga as the official dress for all Roman citizens (1.379). This contract between citizenship and the toga is underscored some sixty years later by Emperor Claudius when trying a Greek accused of appropriating Roman citizenship. Insisting that the defendant wear Greek dress for the prosecution, Claudius allows him to change into the toga for his defense, drawing a strict

---

[6] Walter Benjamin, *Arcades Project,* (Cambridge, MA: Harvard UP, 2002), 460-61.

[7] Roland Barthes, *The Language of Fashion,* trans. Andy Stafford, eds. Andy Stafford and Michael Carter, (Oxford, New York: Berg, 2005), xii.

[8] Marcel Mauss, *The Gift: Expanded Edition,* selected, annotated, and trans. by Jane I. Guyer, foreword Bill Maurer, (Chicago: UP, 2016); and Marcel Mauss, *The Gift,* trans. Ian Cunnison, intro. E. E. Evans-Pritchard, (New York: Norton, 1967).

[9] Erving Goffman, "The Nature of Deference and Demeanor," *American Anthropologist* 58:3 (1956): 475-99; *The Presentation of Self in Everyday Life,* (Garden City, New York: Doubleday, 1959); and *Interaction Ritual* (New York: Doubleday, 1967).

[10] For all references to *The Aeneid,* there is an in-line source (chapter. pages). All other references are footnoted.

correlation between Roman civic status and the right to wear the toga.[11] In the Aeneid, Juno adds a mythological dimension when she insists that Jupiter agrees to maintain the clothing along with the language and customs of the Italians despite the penetration of corrupting Trojans (12. 1114-19). According to Seneca, the Fate Clotho, who speaks of things present, strengthens this stance by saying that Claudius "decided to see all Greeks, Gauls, Spaniards and Britons as toga-clad" thereby equating Empire expansion with the toga.[12]

Congruent with this notable significance that emperors, philosophers, and goddesses award the toga, Quintilian sees the merit of many items of dress as signifiers in Imperial Rome, and documents how emperors wear, shed, and exchange robes, crowns, scepters, etc., to recognize and negotiate power. He reports that in the late first century CE a Roman orator's clothing should be *splendidus et virilism*[13] Clearly, an awareness of non-verbal communication is present here that is consistent with modern capitalist societies where clothing has signifying power, like the robes of U. S. Supreme Court Justices, the red and blue ties worn by Republicans and Democrats, respectively, in the United States, and wigs of English judges.[14] Yet the position held by clothing in antiquity, reinforced by sumptuary legislation like that surrounding the toga

---

[11] Jonathan Edmondson, "Public Dress and Social Control in Late Republican and Early Imperial Rome," (21- 46), in *Roman Dress and the Fabrics of Roman Culture,* Jonathan Edmondson and Alison Keith eds. (Toronto: UP, 2008) 21-2.

[12] T. Corey Brennan, "Tertullian's *De Pallio* and Roman Dress in North Africa," (258-270), in *Roman Dress and the Fabrics,* 258. According to the *Iliad,* even Zeus obeys the Fates command (16.435-70); Ovid, *Metamorphoses,* ed. and trans., Frank Justus Miller, 3rd edn., (Cambridge, Mass.: Harvard UP, 1984) agrees and represents them holding their fabricating tools, and ruling over humans and gods with "iron decrees" (15.781, 799-800).

[13] Glenys Davies, "What Made the Roman Toga *virilis*?" 119-30, in *The Clothed Body in the Ancient World,* Liza Cleland, Mary Harlow and Lloyd Llewellyn-Jones, eds., (Oxford: Oxbow, 2005), 127. See also Augustine, *City of God,* trans. Henry Bettenson, (London: Penguin, 1972, [1467]), who links dress and eternal life with his statement, "All things suitable for clothing and adorning the person are evidence of the peace and glory of immortality" 872.

[14] Scholars who support this position include Reijo Miettinen, "Artifact Mediation in Dewey and in Cultural-Historical Activity Theory," in *Mind, Culture, and Activity* 8:4 (2001): 297-308; Peirce, Philosophical Writings; Grant McCracken, *Culture and Consumption: New Approaches to the Symbolic Character of Consumer Goods and Activities,* (Bloomington: Indiana UP, 1988); Elizabeth Wilson, *Unfolding the Past,* (London: Bloomsbury, 2022) 129, 215-17; Arjun Appadurai, "Commodities and the Politics of Value, (Cambridge: UP, 1988), 3-64; and Jones and Stalleybrass in *Materials of Memory,* among others. See also n.88 above.

cited above, was one of greater power and prominence than that given it today, where other cultural and technological inventions (those using artificial intelligence, for example) vie for ideological and social supremacy in a noisier material world.[15]

Because of this power and prominence assigned to dress in ancient Rome and in the *Aeneid,* I assign to antiquity a tradition that many social theorists convincingly argue for capitalist modernity: that the circulation of dress items transfers social histories and cultural biographies communicating values and emotions inscribed by previous owners.[16] Virgil tracks this circulation through the rituals of gifting and taking. In this way, he entangles past and present, and weaves private into public as he relays ideological and political messages. Augustus supports Virgil financially while writing the *Aeneid,* and this keeps him abreast of current political ambitions. He is also well-schooled in their requirements and often directs dress to this task. This ancient Roman link between dress and politics also respects the claims of a number of modern Western social and cultural theorists.[17]

---

[15] Harlow, "Dress in the Historia Augusta: The Role of Dress in Historical Narrative," in *The Clothed Body in the Ancient World,* (142-153)153, n.98. Here the role of clothing as stored wealth is stressed. According to Cleland, Davis and Lewellyn-Jones, 205, eds. *Greek and Roman Dress from A to Z,* most Greeks and Romans were probably very aware of and competent to access the intrinsic value of particular clothing, as only those with the highest levels of fashion consciousness are today. Thank you to an anonymous reviewer for helping me clarify this point.

[16] For a discussion on the distinction between social histories and cultural biographies see Appadurai 34. For social theorists that advocate similar thesis for modernity see footnote 99.

[17] Scholars such as Appadurai, 3-63; Wilson, 129, 215-17 and 251; Djurdja Bartlett, ed. *Fashion and Politics,* (Yale UP, 2019)1-17: Carol Tulloch, "T-Shirt Matters,"113-35, in *Fashion Knowledge: Theories, Methods, Practices and Politics,* (Bristol: Intellect, 2022); Barbara Vinken, "Fashion, an Oriental Tyranny in the Heart of the West," 61-72, in *Fashion and Politics,* (Yale UP, 2019); Henry Navarro Delgado, "Fashion's Potential to Influence Politics and Culture." CNN Style. 2018, https://www.cnn.com/style/article/fashion-influence-politics-and-culture/index.html /Accessed January 28, 2023; also Victor Davis Hanson writes "...[San Francisco] Bay Area hipsters in ratty clothes are the cool 'good-guys' if they have deep Democratic pockets and talk of 'equity' and 'fairness'... https://amgreatness.com/2022/11/20/the-strange-morality-of-the-bay-area-billionaire-left/ Accessed January 28, 2023 and myself, Linda Matheson, "Imperial Material: Modern Western Fashion Theory and a Seventeenth-Century Eastern Empire," *Dress, the Journal of the Costume Society of America* 37:1 (Oct, 2011): 57-82.

The themes of giving and taking divide this discussion into two parts. Part A focuses on gifts and giving: Aeneas's gifts to Dido (1) A Robe stiff with figures and worked in Gold, (2) A Veil woven round with yellow acanthus flowers, and (3) The Royal scepter. We then discuss Dido's gifts to Aeneas: (1) A Jasper-studded sword hilt and (2) Purple and gold cloaks. Part B focuses on taking via plunder: (1) Euryalus's helmut, (2) Camilla's coveted finery, and (3) Pallas's swordbelt.[18]

Part A: Gifting

Aeneas's Gifts to Dido

Aeneas, the protagonist destined to found Rome, escapes the flames of Troy with a small band of Trojans, who, after being lost at sea and shipwrecked, find safety and welcome at Dido's palace in Carthage. To fulfill the law of *zenia*, the ancient Greek tradition of hospitality, Aeneas offers cherished treasures from Troy as gifts for the Carthaginian Queen.

> Relics of Ilium: a robe stiff with figures
> Worked in gold, and a veil woven round
> With yellow acanthus flowers—both adornments
> Worn by Argive Helen when she sailed
> For Pergamum and her forbidden marriage,
> Marvelous keepsakes of her mother, Leda.
> Along with these a scepter Ilione,
> Eldest of Priam's daughters, once had used.
> A collar hung with pearls and a coronet
> Doubled in gems and gold.
> (1: 883-93).

Aware of the rhetorical power of things and their cultural and political attachments, Virgil links these gifts and their pathos with history and mythology, selecting items that integrate past and present as they suggest future events. Harsh realities of previous owners cling to these gifts, like the sorrows of Leda, Helen of Troy's grieving mother whose tears are the residue of her daughter's

---

[18] *Aeneid,* Virgil, Trans. Robert Fitzgerald, (New York: Random House, 1990) primary translation; also useful *Vergil's Aeneid, A Duel Language Edition,* trans and ed. Joshua W. D. Smith (Bolton, On: Amazon.ca manufacturer, 2017); and *Aeneid,* Virgil. 2002, www.tonykline.co.uk Accessed November 15, 2022.

powerful cross-cultural passion, the kind that enters Dido's life with Aeneas's arrival.[19] Hidden meanings and memories lurk in the richly-embellished folds of Helen's robe, in the leaves of the gold-embroidered acanthus flower on her shimmering veil, and in the glittering blade of the royal Dardanean scepter in which Dido delights. To discover additional meaning that attaches to these gifts, we first turn to etymology.

The word gift derives from the Latin dosis, itself a translation of the Greek term *δοσιζ*; dose or dose of poison. In English, dose can indicate obligation and reciprocity, both of which are germane to the gifting practice. Still, this etymology implies poison too, suggesting that these gifts from the Trojan hero may be fatal to Dido. Both the Latin and the Greek term *dosis* indicate an association of ideas and moral rules attached to gifting.[20] Yet, to understand these, we must consider what we know and what we do not know about these gifts, a paradigm whose very nature asserts tension.

A Robe Stiff with Figures and Worked in Gold

We know that the term robe is from the Latin word palla, and translates as a rectangular outer garment that drapes over a dress.[21] Diverging from the toga in cut, the curved bottom edge is the signifying difference between the two. The word robe is the literary symbol, and to read or speak it is a simple action free of implications; the same for the Latin term palla. However, to consider that this is a "relic[s] of Ilium ...worn by Helen of Troy when she sailed for her forbidden marriage," conjures up visions of the abducted bride, the legendary beauty with the ambiguous reputation (1.883-87). Our mind attaches contextual meaning, and we see the robe's renowned magnificence stained with the blood of Trojan soldiers. Additional meaning comes with the palla's description, as "stiff with figures" and "worked in gold," which indicates embroidery or figures woven in metallic gold thread that stiffens the primary fabric.[22]

---

[19] Allegedly the "abduction" of Helen from Sparta by Paris, King Priam of Troy's son was the cause of the Trojan War, and now we have Dido, another legendary queen and founder of Carthage, who falls in love with a foreigner, the Trojan hero Aeneas.

[20] Mauss, *The Gift,* "Personal and Real Law" (ancient Roman law 146-151). See Jane Guyer's note re the etymology of the word 'gift' 174 n. 122.

[21] Judith Lynn Sebesta and Larissa Bonfante, "Glossary," (241-247), 245; and Henry Bender, "De Habitu Vestis," (146-52), 150. By the time of Imperial Rome, the palla was also worn by some men, but Virgil's use of the term confines it to its initial use for women only.

[22] Harlow, "Historia Augusta," 152, n.10, claims no embroidery exists in the ancient world

Notice the resemblance between the words stiff and straight. The latter term is originally associated with men's garments and good omens, but Roman antiquity appropriates it for the bride's garment because she weaves it while standing straight at an upright or warp-weighted loom. This allows a wider fabric and more voluminous garment.[23] Gold contributes to the garments' stiffness, and we know that at this time, it is woven into fabric. Symbolically mercantile societies bestow enormous power on gold, even those once attributed to magic, and Troy is known for its luxurious gold-embroidered clothing, which it introduces to the Romans through Eastern foreign policy affirming Appaduri's theory that all luxury has a political function.[24]

We also know that this luxurious palla is Helen's and that Helen was a bride because Virgil mentions her forbidden marriage. Through this garment, Virgil associates Helen and Dido, endowing the palla with the symbolism of the fall of the once elegant Troy and the tragic affair between Helen and Paris. Strengthening the symbolism of loss and tragedy, Virgil uses the same garment, the palla, bloodied and torn, on the fiercely foreboding Tisiphone in the underworld (6.746), and yet again to clothe the personification of Discord on Aeneas's shield (8.951). Through this visual montage of the palla, we conclude that Virgil uses it singly and symbolically to communicate disaster and doom.

---

but rather tapestry weave decoration as Homer depicts in the *Iliad* (New York: Farrar, Straus and Giroux, 2004) 3.145-50, in which Helen's tapestry depicts scenes from the Trojan War, and Penelope weaves Laertes's shroud in the *Odyssey*, (New York: Random, 1990), 2.105, 19.152, and 24.142. Alternatively, Cleland, Davis and Lewellyn-Jones eds., *Greek and Roman Dress*, 57, write that "technical considerations and rare fragmentary textiles...show that embroidery was a perfectly available technique...." Congruently Sebesta, "Symbolism in the Costume of Roman Women," in *The World of Roman Costume*, 66, notes archeological evidence provides the remains of a seventh-century BCE woman's garment heavily embroidered in gold found in the Regolini-Galassi tomb.

[23] Sebesta, "Symbolism," 51, n. 18; and Laetitia La Follette, "The Costume of the Roman Bride," (54-64) in *The World of Roman Costume*, 55. Also Kelly Olsen, 21-24.

[24] Sebesta, "Symbolism" 66, notes archeological evidence from the 7th c BCE provides fragments of a purple linen tunic or shroud mixed with bits of gold found in a funerary urn of the same century from Chianciano; and in the *Aeneid*, Andromache gives Ascanius "cloth of gold" (3.644), and the mother of young Lausus, a soldier killed in battle, weaves him a shirt of the same (10.1044-55). Other examples in the same text are (1.892), and (4.359). Gold was lavishly used in the Imperial periods, usually woven into wool. For the politics of gold see Appadurai, "Commodities and the Politics of Value," 3; for its power see Barthes, *The Language of Fashion*, 60.

Despite its beauty and richness, its literary associations make it a thought-provoking gift for Dido. Now, on to what we do not know.

Not known is the primary fiber from which this glittering garment, first worn by Argive Helen and now gifted to Dido, is woven. Wool is the fiber of choice in ancient Greece and the only one that women card, spin, or weave in Homer, and it is the favorite of Augustus, who wears a woolen toga with undershirts of the same fiber.[25] But linen, or fine cloth as it is known, is also used for women's clothing, particularly dresses called peploi, which in the Odyssey and the Iliad can be highly decorated treasures held in storehouses. One such treasure made by Helen herself is described as "[so] brilliant with embroidery...it shimmered like a star."[26] Thucydides reports that linen takes about three times as long to produce as wool; hence, a luxury, which in Homer's world is confined to female clothes where it marks gender and status.[27] Yet the palla that Virgil refers to is an outer robe and counterpart to the Greek himation, which functions to protect; consequently, I suggest that the robe Aeneas gives Dido is woven not with linen but with fine wool, which while allowing luxury supplies greater protection from inclement weather.

Consistent with this choice of fiber is Dido's deathbed allusion to wool's ascribed apotropaic character when she warns her sister Anna and Barce, her dead husband's nurse, to "put on pure wool around your brow" to avert (any more) evil influences (4.885-886); and later we see the holy headband, the sacred woolen fillet that binds the head of the priest Haemonides (10.756-759). Hippocrates also supports this choice in his documentation of the belief in the exclusive relationship between women and wool in ancient Greece and Rome. It compares the woman's body to wool, loose in texture and hydrophilic, retaining more moisture than a man's body. And finally, wool also functions in mythology as a metonym for what biologically makes a woman a woman: the womb. When Hephaistos fails to rape the virgin Goddess Athena, his semen falls on her leg. She uses a tuft of wool to wipe it off and then throws it to the ground on the exact spot where Erikhthonios is immediately born. The wool

---

[25] Sebesta, "Tunica Ralla, Tunica Spissa," 72. Also Clausen, 55 mentions Dido's smooth woolen napkins, and the sacred white woolen fillet that binds the priest Haemonides head to great effect 10.756-759.

[26] *Odyssey*, 15.124-6.

[27] Hans van Weiss, "Trailing Tunics and Sheepskin Coats: Dress and Status in Early Greece," in *The Clothed Body*, 45. *Odyssey*, 4.793, 6.31, 6.43, 13.83, 17.65, 23.183.

acts as a substitute womb for Athena, who coincidently holds the title Goddess of Weaving.[28]

Since Helen's weaving is as legendary as her other activities, she may have woven the fabric for this beautiful keepsake of her mother, Leda, now gifted to Dido. This is speculation, but if true, the possibility exists of more detailed, even poisonous personal histories clinging to its golden folds. The tension between what is known and what is reasoned speculation increases the mystery in the meanings that attach to this gift and that entangle the second, Helen's embroidered veil.[29]

A Veil Woven round with Yellow Acanthus Flowers

This veil that gleams with golden acanthus flowers is the second luxurious article of Helen's that Virgil selects for a gift to Dido. Because it is another cherished memento of Leda, and the most distinctive element of traditional Roman bridal attire, it probably is Helen's wedding veil. This matters because, despite scholarly differences on the precise use of the veil in antiquity, there is agreement on the use of the *flammeum* or wedding veil. It is described as diaphanous and beautiful, with its yellow-orange color hailing from the saffron plant, a plant useful to women as it provides medicine for menstrual problems.[30] Substantiating this connection, one Juvenal scholar calls the color of the gold-embroidered veil bloodlike, which is presumably pink-gold.[31] Scholars debate whether the flammeum was red or yellow, but Pliny the Elder sides with the later writing, "I understand that yellow was the first color to be highly esteemed and was granted as an exclusive privilege to women for their

[28] Judith Lynn Sebesta, "Visions of Gleaming Textiles and a Clay Core: Greek Women and Pandora," in *Women's Dress in the Ancient Greek World*, ed. Lloyd Lewellyn-Jones, (Swansea: Classical Press of Wales 2002), 125-142, especially 132.

[29] *Iliad*, 3.145-50, tells us that Helen weaves like most aristocratic women of her era. See also the *Odyssey*, 2.105, 19.152, and 24.142 for Penelope weaves as a ruse to keep her suitors at bay. Also I. David Jenkins, "The Ambiguity of Greek Textiles," in *Arethusa* 18.2 (1985): 109-132, tells us that in *The Oresteia*, Clytemnestra weaves two tapestries which she uses to murder Agamemnon; and in *Euripides* Medea weaves a poisoned robe that she sends her rival Jason's new love interest.

[30] La Follette, "Roman Bride," 55. The ancients equated the phrase "to cloud over" with "to veil." The Latin word for "cloud" is *nubes* and links to the verb *nubere*, "to be married." The bride's head is veiled or "clouded over."

[31] Sebesta, "Symbolism," 48.

bridal veils."[32] This becomes a noteworthy quotation given the use of yellow clothing later in Virgil's epic. Remember, its exclusiveness and honored use for brides renders it inappropriate for other uses.

The golden acanthus flowers relate their own stories. The Roman writer Vitruvius (75 -15 BCE) relates that the sight of acanthus flowers growing in a votive basket on the grave of a young girl inspired Callimachus, a Greek architect and sculptor, to use them to create the Corinthian decor. In Christian traditions, some acanthus species are equated with Christ's crown of thorns and ideas of sin, punishment, and repentance. Compared to flowers that represent love, happiness, and gratitude, the acanthus blossom withers, but in the language of flowers, they represent fine art and artifice.[33] These are provocative ideas to ponder in relation to Helen's, now Dido's wedding veil.

The function of this enveloping rectangular Greek bridal veil, probably the prototype for the Roman version, is to protect the bride from evil spirits and obscenity during the passage from her father's to her husband's home.[34] Helen's ambiguous past, however, confuses this issue of innocence and need for protection, for as Virgil infers, these gifts accompany her willing abduction from her husband King Menelaus's home in Sparta to her new home with Prince Paris in Troy.

We know from the Iliad, ashamed of leaving her husband Menelaus and causing the Trojan War, Helen uses a veil to conceal her tears. In an act of modesty, shame, or grief, she covers her head with silvery veils before exiting her chamber for the battlements of Troy, demonstrating at least one of the multivalent meanings of veiling in ancient Greek society.[35] See Figure 3.1.

---

[32] La Follette, "Roman Bride," 55.

[33] Wilhelmina Feemster Jashemski, Frederick G. Meyer and Massimo Ricciardi, "Plants: Evidence from Wall Paintings, Mosaics, Sculpture, Plant Remains, Graffiti, Inscriptions and Ancient Authors," in *The Natural History of Pompeii, Vol.1.* 1st Ed. 80-180, edited by Wilhelmina Feemster, (Cambridge: UP, 2002); and https://www.secretflowerlanguage.com /Flower/Acanthus, (accessed January 11, 2023).

[34] Sebesta, "Symbolism," 48

[35] *Iliad,* 3.165-70; Sebesta, "Symbolism," 48; Edwards, "Aspects of Costume in Josephus," (153-159) tell us that according to literary and numismatic evidence the symbolic significance of veils "was associated with law, morality, social responsibility and morning" 155; See also Douglas L. Carins, "The Meaning of the Veil in Ancient Greek Culture," (73-93), in *Women's Dress in the Ancient Greek World*; Croom, 112; Olsen, 21-22; Sebesta, "Visions of Gleaming Textiles," 135; Robert Francis Murphy, *Social Distance and*

Figure 3.1: Helen and Priam at the Scaen Gate

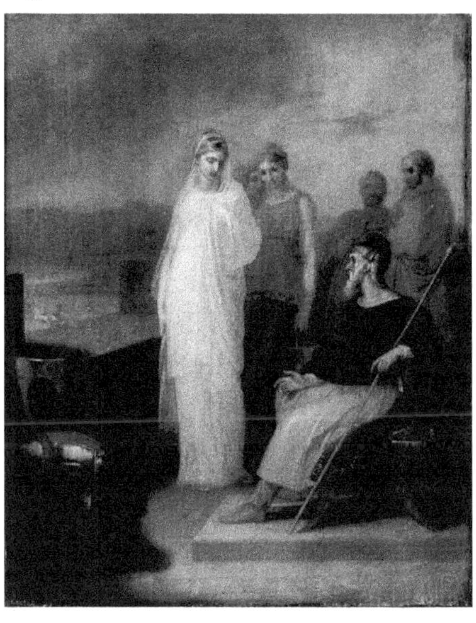

Richard Cook, British 1808 (1784–1857); oil on canvas; 29.3 x 24 cm; 11.53 x 9.4 in; Digital image file no.16286; Source File no. FPa75; Folger Shakespeare Library Digital Image; https://commons.wikimedia.org/wiki/Template:PD-1996 (accessed January 10, 2023).

Besides modesty, shame, or grief, other catalysts for veiling are pollution and religious rituals. The common denominator is that the veil marks a sense of separation and indicates that status is in question, like Helen's status, which King Priam, Paris's father, may be probing in Figure 3.1, or Penelope's, in the Odyssey when in silky veils she addresses the suitors who pressure her to marry.[36] Goffman calls these strategies of interaction states of "demeanor" and "deference," and they include (1) a sense of "sacred self," our personal identity, and (2) "ideal public self," to which we are committed, and which all rituals of social presentation are designed to protect.[37] Veiling happens when one's sacred or public self is challenged or threatened, as with both Helen and Penelope, and this will soon be the case with Dido.

---

the Veil (London: Berg, 1999); Martha Nussbaum, "Veiled Threats" *The New York Times*, Opinionator, July 11, 2010, (accessed January 27, 2023); and Wallach J. Scott, *The Politics of the Veil.* Princeton, NJ: Princeton UP, 2007.

[36] Carins, "The Meaning of the Veil" 73-93; *Odyssey,* 1.353.

[37] Goffman, *Interaction Ritual* 44; and "Deference and Demeanor," 475-99.

Figure 3.2: *Venus Appears to Aeneas on the Shores of Carthage*

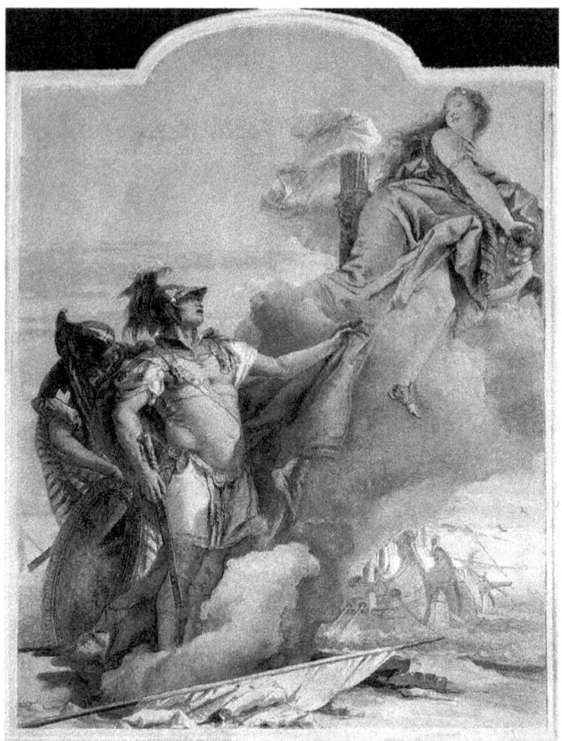

Giovanni Battista Tiepolo, Italian 1757 (1696-1770); fresco; 230 x 180 cm; 90.5 x 70.75 in; Villa Valmarana, Vicenza. The fresco depicts both a cloud and a garment extending from Venus to Aeneas. Credit: Web Gallery of Art https://commons.wikimedia.org/wiki/Template: PD-1996 (accessed January 15, 2023).

Virgil frequently uses veils to separate and shield his characters until the environment is ready to receive them with appropriate deference and a fitting demeanor. One translation of the *Aeneid* in which the word veil appears eighteen times underscores his repetitious use of this technique.[38] Interestingly, the majority of Virgil's veilings are metaphorical and employ words like mist or cloud, which further emphasize his reliance on the practice.[39] In one example, the goddess Venus, Aeneas's mother, veils her son in a cloud presented as an amictus,

---

[38] Virgil: *The Aeneid*, 2002, PIT Poetry in Translation www.tonykline.co.uk.acc. November 15, 2022.

[39] See note 115 for the etymological link between veils and clouds.

a toga-like garment, to enable him to enter Carthage undetected (1.563-66 and 598-99). This garment is metaphorically both a natural and supernatural cover as it links the image of a cloud to clothing that veils and protects Aeneas until the time is right for Dido and her court to receive him.[40]

The cloud veils Aeneas as he enters Carthage, and shrouds him all the way to the Temple of Juno, where he first meets Dido. Note how artist Johann Tischbein (1722-1789) interprets this meeting (Figure 3.3) to show the cloud dissipating behind Aeneas's head in the upper right quadrant of the canvas.

Figure 3.3: *Aeneas before Dido*

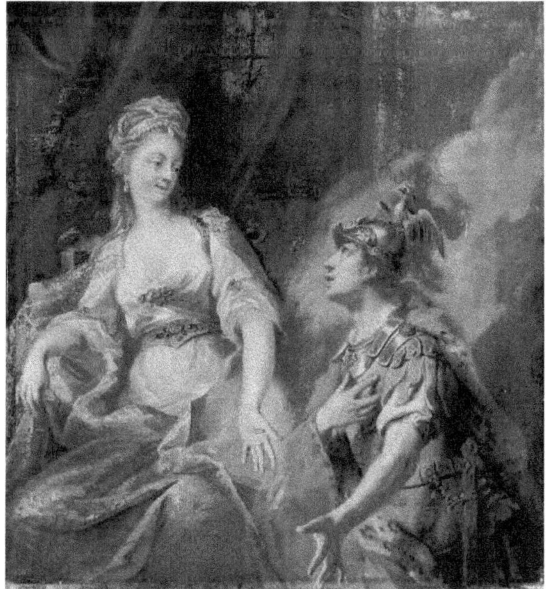

Johann Heinrich Tischbein, German 1773 (1722-1789); Oil on canvas; 62.5 x 68.5 cm; 24.6 x26.9 in; https://datenbank.museum-kassel.de/28523; https://commons.wikimedia.org /wiki/Template:PD-1996 (accessed January 16, 2023).

Nicolas Verkolye (1673-1746), in his early eighteenth-century painting (Figure 3.4), depicts this same first encounter where Dido welcomes some of Aeneas's fellow Trojans. He, too, portrays a cloud at our Trojan hero's feet, lower right

[40] Liza Cleland, Glenis Davis and Lloyd Lewellyn-Jones. eds. *Greek and Roman Dress,* 5; and Bender, "De Habitu Vestis," 149.

quadrant, which dissolves when Dido asks to see their king and Aeneas reveals his identity (1.797-800). He waits for the appropriate moment to shed his veil when the Queen and her attendants are ready to receive him with fitting esteem; thus, he protects both his private and public identities.

Figure 3.4: *Dido and Aeneas*

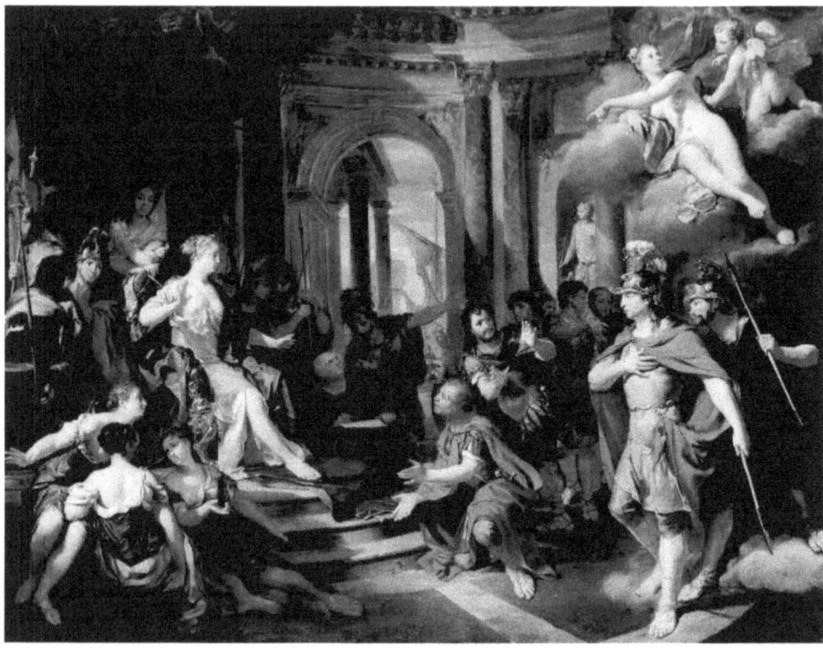

Nicolas Verkolye, Dutch, c early eighteenth-century; (1673-1746); oil on canvas; 90.2 × 117.5 cm; 35 1/2 × 46 1/4 in; Acc no. 71. PA.66; Source: The J. Paul Getty Museum, Los Angeles; https://commons.wikimedia.org/wiki/Template:PD-1996 (accessed January 18, 2023).

Besides following Goffman, this scenario agrees with Mauss, whom Keith Hart describes as trying "to define our individuality while belonging in subtle ways to others."[41] Aeneas remains veiled while he defines himself before interacting with others. Nor did Verkoyle forget the mythological dimension; observe Venus meddling from her cloud at the top right of the canvas.

---

[41] Bill Maurer, "Foreword," in *The Gift* (2016), xv.

Helen's veil suggests separation and change of status for its new owner, yet in the nature of veils, it blurs the reasons for this. One of the great tragic heroines of Western literature, Dido is beautiful, wealthy, loved, admired, and accomplished. She is the reigning queen of a prosperous kingdom that she establishes after being thrust from her land of birth by her treacherous brother Pygmalion. Virgil employs this veil and the palla as agents of change because they carry components of Helen's life, which Dido is about to absorb: passion, tragedy, and an ambiguous memory. Allegedly causing the Trojan War by her willing abduction and love of a foreigner - the kind of love in which Dido is about to engage with Aeneas - Helen signals the quest for undying fame, a position already won by Dido in founding Carthage, the third most sophisticated city in the Roman Empire.

On the one hand, Helen helps Odysseus spy on Troy, and on the other, she thwarts the Greek plot to conquer by the ruse of the Horse; the kind of ambiguity that we see in Aeneas's actions towards Dido, to whom he pledges undying love and shared governance of her Kingdom, yet pursues his destiny to found Rome. [42] Helen's close association with Aphrodite, whose threats are as terrible as her gifts are desirable, reveals her as menacing yet irresistible. The same applies to Aeneas in regard to his gifts and faithlessness to Dido. Finally, Helen's fame in legend and in literature derives from being raped. Besides her lawful husband, she has been with Paris, Theseus, Enarsphoros, Deiphobos, Achilles, and Proteus.[43] Even if there are artistic elaborations and the motif of rape traditional for all known consorts of the goddess, the fact, as far as myth allows fact, is rape.[44] Ultimately, by having Aeneas honor and decorate Dido with gifts intimately associated with Helen, our ancient bard infers this ideological issue of rape as a potential epitaph for the Carthaginian Queen and associates the unfamiliar etymology of the term gift, poison, more closely to his narrative.

Virgil endows Aeneas with little compassion for Helen. In fact, he harbors murderous thoughts of her, "a hated thing" and "that Fury both to her homeland and Troy." When he sees her trying to hide in Priam's kingdom, a "fire blazed up" within him wishing to punish her and avenge his city (2.745-756).

---

[42] Linda Lee Clader, *Helen: The Evolution from Divine to Heroic in Greek Epic Tradition,* (Leiden, the Netherlands: E. J. Brill, 1976), 81.

[43] Calder, *Helen,* 71.

[44] Calder, *Helen,* 71- 2.

Figure 3.5: *Venus prevents her son Aeneas from killing Helen of Troy*

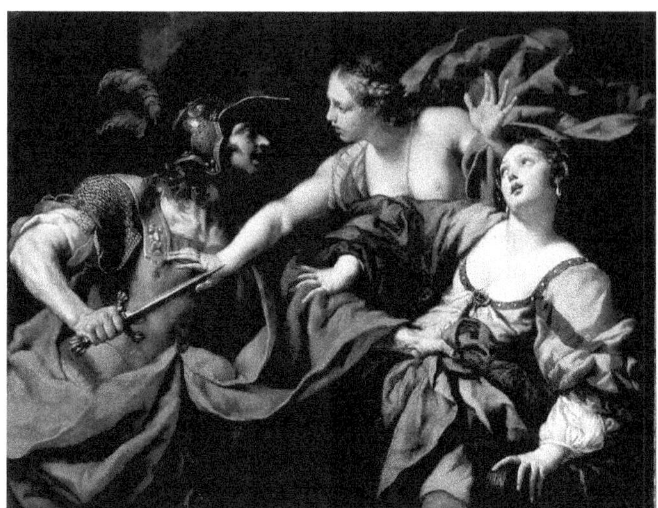

Luca Ferrari, Italian c.1650 (1605-1654); oil on canvas; 128.3 x 169.5 cm; 50.51 x 66.73 in; acc. no.1460; Art Gallery of South Australia; https://en.wikipedia.org/wiki/en:Libraryof Congress (accessed January 18, 2023).

As Lucca Ferreri demonstrates in Figure 3.5, Venus restrains him from this act of extreme violence with the clarity of divine and human reason. Why do we ask? Does Aeneas give Dido gifts associated with someone for whom he feels such contempt? At the time this epic was being written, the *palla* plus the *flammeum,* together with a metal collar, traditionally hung with pearls, comprised the Roman bridal costume, so Aeneas gave Dido gifts associated with the Roman bride. We know that before founding Carthage, Dido was a bride herself who pledged her husband, Sychaeus, for her undying love. Sadly, he was slain by Pygmalion, and despite this pledge, she is about to become a bride again.[45] Aeneas's gifts forecast that this marriage will end in tragedy. Ironically, Virgil tells us other gifts are available. Besides other royal treasures from Troy, a holy diadem and embroidered purple robe(s) (9.326-32), silver and more richly woven robes from Helenus and Andromache, and a gold-embroidered Meliboean crimson cloak are all potential presents. Despite these

---

[45] Clausen, 211, tells us that Dido was married for the first time and only briefly to Sychaeus (no children) and is newly arrived in North Africa. Virgil imagines her as the daughter of a dynastic Roman Royal family who would, like Julia, Augustus's daughter, have married at about age fourteen.

seemingly more appropriate choices, Virgil chooses to have his pious protagonist offer gifts that belong to a woman who, although idolized by some, is scorned by many, including the gift-giver.

By choosing Helen's clothing, Virgil appropriates her personal story, exposes it to public levels, and associates it with Dido. This agrees with Mauss's hypothesis that obligatory gifts or reciprocal dues "are fictitious expressions of the movement of personalities and the objects confounded with them."[46] Helen of Troy is a resounding personality in mythology and literature, and these gifts that represent her life are symbolic gestures of decoration and honor as well as dominance and control. With them, Virgil marries themes of myth, history, and ideology with the passionate and bloodletting formation of the Italian race. His micro-level stories involving gifted articles of attire express questions of macro-level significance. He ties Helen's actions and the destruction of Troy to Dido's personal tragedy, as well as Carthage to the founding of the Roman Empire, and he entangles these themes through the telling threads of dress.

Ilione's scepter - the physical sword that wreaks psychological havoc- previously used by Priam's eldest daughter is another example of this dress-narrative technique, and the final gift from Aeneas to Dido.

The Royal Scepter

In the first blush of love, Dido delights in this scepter, yet ultimately chooses it to kill herself when Aeneas abandons her to the wrath of her once beloved citizens, who now see her as a traitor. Unchanged in physical form, this sword that once brought the glow of affection to her cheek now "gives pain quietus with [its] steel blade" when suicide becomes the only option (4.759888-89). As painter Andrea Sacchi (1599-1661) adeptly illustrates (Figure 3.6) in his *Death of Dido,* it is the emotional intensity etched in the blade that is pivotal to the narrative.

The scepter, intended to function as a prized token from the lost kingdom of her beloved, shifts to the weapon of destruction for an agonized Carthaginian queen: "A gift desired once for no such need," whispers Dido as she climbs the pyre and plunges the Dardan sword into her heart (4.898-899, 921-922). By constituting an indexical representation of Aeneas, the Dardan sword adopts a special use, and transforms from a royal relic to a scythe for suicide. Besides the

---

[46] Mauss, *The Gift,*1967, 47.

scepter, other dress items are featured in Dido's death scene. She voices her last words to Aeneas's garments, see the armor lower left, which represents another index, while her sister Anna, not featured here, uses her torn clothing to absorb the blood.[47] For Anna with her woolen fillet on her head, see Figure 3.7 by Belgian painter Joseph Stallaert (1825-1903). While still featuring the sword and armor, this one evokes a more Egyptian feeling in both clothing and décor, evoking a Cleopatra comparison.

Figure 3.6: *Death of Dido*

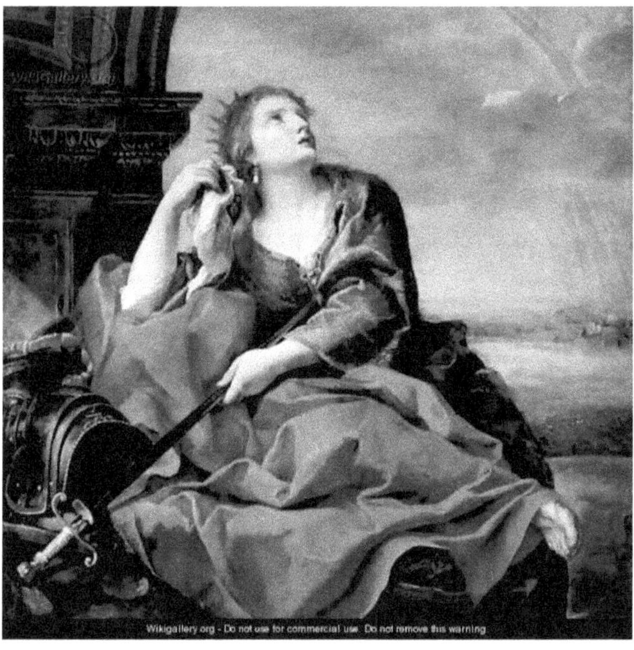

Andrea Sacchi, Italian, c. early seventeenth-century (1599-1661); *oil on canvass;* 148 × 140 cm; 58.2 × 55.1 in; Musée des Beaux-Art de Caen; https://commons.wikimedia.org/wiki/Template:PD-1996 (accessed January 25, 2023).

[47] Charles S. Peirce, "Scientific Metaphysics," in *Collected Papers of Charles Sanders Peirce,* Vol.6, ed. Charles Hartshorne and Paul Weiss, (Cambridge, MA: Harvard UP, 1935) 272-77. An *index* stands in for and has a direct connection with the thing it represents; see also Bender, "De Habitu Vestis,"147; Contra Barthes, *Language of Fashion,* 12, suggests that "the notion of index is itself ambiguous. He asks if vestimentary form is really ...produced outside of any intention"?

Figure 3.7: *The Death of Dido*

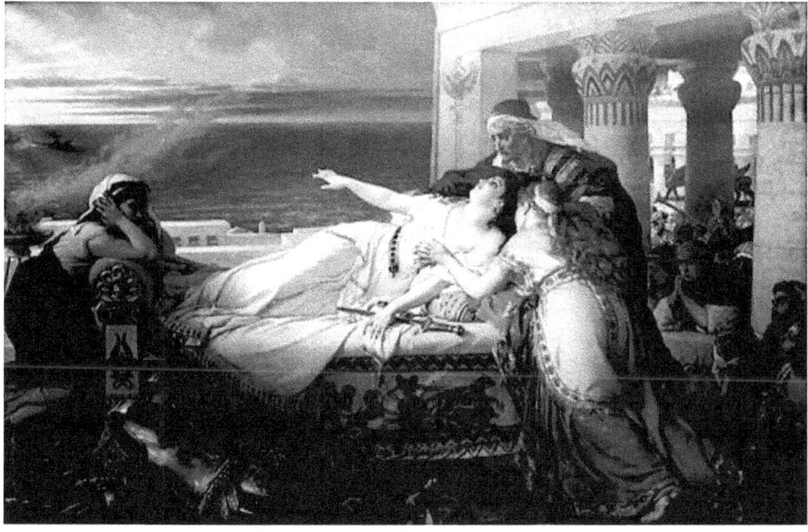

Joseph Stallaert, Belgian 1872, (1825-1903); oil on canvass; 265 x 412 cm; 104.3 x 162.2 in; no. 2522; Royal Museums of Fine Arts of Belgium, Brussels; https://commons.wikimedia.org/wiki/Template:PD-1996 (accessed January 25, 2023).

Dress items entangle Dido's life and death, which completes this first section on her gifts, but before discussing those to Aeneas, her paradoxical position merits a few words.

With Dido, Virgil presents a paradox. Fundamentally opposite to the male, pious and dutiful proto-Roman hero Aeneas, or Augustus, and unlike other epic women, she is a fully developed character with a thriving kingdom before Aeneas even arrives in Carthage (1.576-594). She exudes strength, beauty, and, most of all, foreignness that invokes Cleopatra, whose legacy is recent and still consumes Rome with ambiguous loathing. She, too, is the hero's lover, a queen with loyal followers. Because Dido's formula of femininity is unacceptable to the Roman authority, she challenges the notions of leadership as well as the patriarchal Roman society. By placing personal emotions before state matters, she signals subversiveness and even danger to a Roman readership. Choosing suicide, she aggravates the epic norm by addressing the clothes of her unfaithful husband and using his sword as an implement of her death, making it obvious that the supposed hero of this epic, the Trojan prince, causes her death as clearly as if he wielded the sword with his own hands. Now, we move to the gifts that these suspect hands receive.

Dido's Gifts to Aeneas

> With a withering glance, Jupiter observes Aeneas wearing Dido's gifts, and dispatches Mercury to chastise him for loitering in Carthage and neglecting his mandate to found Rome.
> He noted well the sword hilt the man wore,
> Adorned with yellow jasper; and the cloak
> Aglow with Tyrian dye upon his shoulders—
> Gifts of the wealthy queen, who had interwoven
> Gold thread in the fabric (4.355-59).

We discover that these gifts from the Sidonian queen are highly nuanced. One of the nuances is their foreignness, which ignites the Roman dislike of foreign dress, and so when Jupiter sees Aeneas "ablaze in a cloak of Tyrian purple" from Dido's native land, he considers it an unworthy spectacle.[48] The luxury of the purple interwoven with gold is also problematic, as the association between luxuria and corruption is always close. Additionally, the wearing of costly and inappropriate dress suggests excessive behaviors in other areas.[49] Along with the purple and gold cloak, which we will discuss later, the sword-hilt embellished with gemstones also prompts a sharp retort from Mercury.

A Jasper-Studded Sword Hilt

Barthes describes the gemstone as long participating in the power game, that of a terrific power that it demonstrates simply by being seen.[50] Jasper is no exception. It is a favored gem in the ancient world and a storied one. The term jasper has many derivations: from Old French jaspre, from Latin iaspis, from Ancient Greek *ἴασπις* (iaspis), and ultimately (via an oriental language) from Persian (yašp). [51] Denoting a spotted or speckled stone, it is usually red, yellow, brown, or green; and when highly polished, it is used for ornamentation for items such as vases, seals, snuffboxes, and sword belts. Relatively translucent,

---

[48] Clausen, 13, n. 29; for Roman dislike of foreign dress see Richard Oliver, Allen Marcus Lyne, *Words and the Poet: Characteristic Techniques of Style in Vergil's Aeneid,* (Oxford: UP, 1989), 188-9; Edward Gibbon, *The History of the Decline and Fall of the Roman Empire,* (London: Strahan and Cadell, 1776-1789), ch 27.
[49] Harlow, "*Historia Augusta,*"147.
[50] Barthes, *Language of Fashion,* 60.
[51] https://www.yourdictionary.com/jasper; From American Heritage Dictionary of the English Language 5th ed. and Wiktionary, (accessed November 18, 2022).

these embedded gemstones gleam in the sunlight, evoking richness to the belt and to its wearer. However, ambiguity is at work here, as at this time in Rome, jewels worn by men can be perceived to denigrate character and question moral authority and leadership ability, implying effeminateness and love of richness over rulership. Yet Virgil may be directing us beyond richness to a moral question that Egyptologist archeologist Flinders Petrie raises: That the Tarshish, the tenth stone on the Hebrew High Priest's Breastplate, is yellow jasper. This implies that Aeneas is the High Priest of Dido's kingdom, an exalted position she creates for him. [52] This priestly association strengthens with Dido's second gift, the purple cloak interwoven with gold thread, a garment that signals a high level of social status, among other things.[53]

A Purple Cloak Woven with Gold

The cloak that Dido makes and gives to Aeneas is a laena, which, according to Suetonius, is a double sized toga, and one of the other things it signals is that it is customarily worn by priests when performing sacrifice. Virgil references the laena only once in the Aeneid, and uses its religious implication to show how disoriented and isolated from his mission Aeneas has become.[54] Its critical significance lies in its association with sacrifice, however, and links to Dido's forthcoming suicide: the ultimate human sacrifice, and a crucial element in the entire epic that inspired its adoption by writers like Ovid, Dante, Chaucer, Marlowe, and Spencer.[55]

---

[52] Sir William Matthews Flinders Petrie, "Egypt," in *Encyclopedia Britannica, Vol 15, 11th ed.* (Cambridge: UP, 1911), 279.

[53] Cited in Michael Koortbojian, "Costumes and their Symbolism at Rome," in *Roman Dress and the Fabrics of Roman Culture,* (81-94), 82. Pliny acknowledges that in Rome at this time appearance matters, and recognizes its role to signal status and hierarchy. To significant extent the image of the person not only represents but also creates the reality of the person.

[54] Bender, "De Habitu Vestis," 150,151, n. 16. Phyllis Tortora and Keith Eubank, *Survey of Historic Costume,* (New York: Fairchild, 2001), 76. Tortora and Eubank define the *laena* as a circle of cloth folded to a semicircle, which is thrown over the shoulders and pinned at the front.

[55] Ovid, *Heroides In Heroides and Amores,* ed. Grant Showerman, (London: William Heinemann, 1931); Dante Alighieri, *The Inferno* (New York: Random, 2010); Geoffrey Chaucer, "The House of Fame," in *The Concise Oxford Companion to English Literature,* 3rd ed. Margaret Drabble, Jenny Stringer, and Daniel Hahn eds., (Oxford: UP, 2007); Christopher Marlowe, *Dido, Queen of Carthage* (New York: Random, 1983); Edmund Spencer, *The Faerie Queene* (New York: Penguin, 1979); to list a few.

Yet, the cloak slung on Aeneas's shoulders has other involvements. Its royal purple dye comes from the murex shellfish in the Phoenician city of Tyre, the capital of Dido's homeland in the eastern Mediterranean, which, with Sidon, is known for yielding the most beautiful purple in antiquity. These nuanced purple threads bearing Dido's personal history and cultural biography entwine with gold to fabricate Aeneas's cloak.

The fashion trend for purple hues, from violet to scarlet, is not lost on Virgil, who adorns his text with both the Tyrian and Trojan tints. [56] Some examples follow: Enhancing the golden radiance of the hunt where Juno arranges her unhallowed marriage, Dido wears a purple and gold embroidered Sidonian *chlamys* over a scarlet and gold dress (4.191- 4). Aeneas, too, is clad in scarlet and gold for the hunt and has two additional purple/gold cloaks that Dido fashions for him, the laena and the amictus (4.356-59 and 11.96-103). Aeneas sends "the embroidered purple... woven by Trojan women" to King Latinus (7.325-332; 7.335-336), who responds by presenting his finest horses ornamented with purple saddle-cloths to the Trojans (7.376-378). Pliny the Elder records the spectacular uses of this preferred pigment when he writes that "[t]he rods and axes of Rome clear a path to the color purple: it marks the honorable status of boyhood; it distinguishes the senator from the knight; it is called in to secure the favor of gods, and it adds radiance to every garment, while in a triumphal robe it is blended with gold."[57] Homer also employs the word porphuros, but not with the brightness of Virgil's use, rather with sometimes sinister overtones.[58] Although Virgil's brightness enchants and distracts us when worn by Dido on the hunt and when adorning Aeneas's shoulders as he loiters triumphant in his governing role at Carthage, its

---

[56] P*urpura*, Latin origin of the word purple, is the name given to a shellfish that yields the famous Tyrian dye, which was more like magenta or fuchsia than what is now called purple. Turner Wilcox, *The Mode in Costume* (New York: Scribner's Sons, 1958 [1942]), 19. For further discussion of purple see Meyer Reinhold, *History of Purple as a Status Symbol in Antiquity,* (Brussels: Latomus Revue d' Études Latines, 1970); and Sebesta, "Tunica Ralla, Tunica Spissa," 65-76.

[57] Luce Boulnois, *Silk Road,* (Hong Kong: Odyssey Books, 2001) 109-10.

[58] Johnson, *Darkness Visible,* 69. Also Harlow, "Historia Augustus" notes that "Gallienus (253-68 AD) is derided for appearing in a purple cloak (*chlamys)*with jeweled and golden fibulae 'at Rome where emperors always wear the toga,'" 147.

brightness diminishes with its use in the amictus that unites with another purple/gold chlamys to veil Pallas's hair before it is set aflame. As a shroud for the ill-fated body of this beloved son whose safety Aeneas too rashly promises, the radiance of the gold dims to a dull yellow (11.96-103). This suggests that Virgil is sophisticated in his use of the signals of dress, including its color trends. This ends our discussion of Dido's gifts to Aeneas, but before we leave, one more gift from Anchesis, Aeneas's father, begs acknowledgment because of its cultural authority.

When Aeneas flees Carthage and Dido's pyre, he enlists the Arcadians' help to fulfill his destiny. Their loyalty was secured years before by a gold-embroidered chlamys that Aeneas's Father, Anchises, gave King Evander. A rectangular woolen mantle woven in Troy, the chlamys is a forerunner of the generals' cloak, the paludamentum, which indicates leadership. Evander's son Prince Pallas, now the leader, wears it when he goes to war and dies in it. Yet Harlow's research in the Historica Augustus tells us that the chlamys is an ambiguous garment, which, besides participating in leadership, can "indicate a rejection or failure to recognize traditional Roman values."[59] This ambiguity becomes pertinent when we recall that Virgil chooses to clothe Dido in a chlamys for the hunt during which her disastrous marriage takes place. The chlamys woven by Dido that Aeneas uses as a shroud or veil for Pallas's body is therefore provocative.

The veiling here is protective and provocative. The coverings from Carthage shroud the body of Pallas, erecting a boundary between the flames and the handsome youth. This shroud cites an unstable union built on complexities, contradictions, and ambiguities. It ties Dido to Pallas and funeral pyre to funeral pyre as it recalls the fires of Troy. All the while it announces contesting themes of individual and state, creation and destruction. Troy burns, but Dido saves the Trojan Aeneas, who founds Rome, yet deserts her. Furthermore, Dido creates Carthage, which falls under the Roman Empire. Pallas is a casualty of the founding of this Empire, and the ambiguous chlamys questions all of their leadership skills. In this way, Virgil directs items of attire to tie people and countries together as he probes Roman practices of patriarchy and governance. He selects, transforms, and adapts items of dress to the need at hand. Far from frivolous fashion, these gifts honor life's achievements and question death's destruction.

---

[59] Harlow, "Historia Augustus," 146.

Although Dido's gifts of embroidered purple and gold speak visual volumes, an "accursed sword-belt" at the epic's end echoes her first gift to Aeneas, the jasper-studded sword hilt. This item is the ultimate catalyst that causes Aeneas to kill Turnus, his worthy opponent, and ends the epic with the theme of taking (12.1282). This brings us to Part B, where Virgil perpetuates more questions via the taking/plunder scenario.

Part B: Taking

Like gifting, taking circulates and transfers material objects; it puts them in motion and invigorates them with social and cultural context. Here, the focus is on armor, whose repeating motif begins in Troy when the Trojans don Greek armor taken from slain Greek soldiers. By this, they hope to infiltrate enemy ranks and steal an easy victory. However, by assuming the identity of the Greeks, they put themselves in peril from their fellow Trojans who fail to recognize them. The misidentification proves fatal, and the armor of dead Greeks becomes the armor of dead Trojans (2.542-44).[60] Taking, or plunder, is thus more complex and problematic than it first appears, and Virgil masterfully employs dress to illustrate this. The following examples highlight some of these complexities, when armor itself becomes a device to structure, mold, and advance the story while covertly questioning accepted but often destructive practices of empire-building. As with gifting, these items carry and convey personal biographies and political histories, recalling past actions while performing present tasks. A young soldier's helmet is our first illustration.

Euryalus's Helmet

The proudly plundered helmet that crowns Euryalus's youthful head blends history, mythology, and reality with a repetitious rhythm. Given by the rich man Caedicus to Remulus, and at his death passed on to his grandson Euryalus, who in victory takes it from Messapus's slain body, the epic's framing reveals how this storied helmet transforms prized plunder into the article of betrayal for the

---

[60] Hector defeats Patroclus and absconds with his armor in the *Iliad*, yet he kills the unknown man to possess his armor in *Troilus and Cressida*. It is when Hector is still putting on the armor from this unknown man that he is killed by Achilles and his Myrmidons. See the *Iliad*, and William Shakespeare, *Troilus and Cressida*, (261- 324) ed. Kenneth Palmer, in *the Arden Shakespeare* (London: Methuen, 1982). Jones and Stalleybrass offer an excellent discussion of this misidentification through plunder and disguise 257.

soldier who would have gone unseen but for the shimmering rays of moonlight that the helmet reflects (9.504 -15). Further problems result when the weight of other plunder he carries slackens the speed of his escape. Fearful and confused, his enemy reels him down. (9.543-44).

> Euryalus's helmet
> In the clear night's half-darkness had betrayed him
> Glimmering back, as he had not foreseen,
> Dim rays of moonlight. And the horsemen took,
> Sharp notice of that sight (9.526-30).
> Deep night under the boughs, and weight of booty,
> Slowed Euryalus and fear confused him (9.543-4).
>
> Euryalus In death went reeling down,
> And blood streamed on his handsome length, his neck
> Collapsing let his head fall on his shoulder—
> As a bright flower cut by a passing plough
> Will droop and wither slowly, or a poppy
> Bow its head upon its tired stalk
> When overborne by a passing rain (9.613-19).

Virgil contrasts the poppy's delicate beauty with the harsh ugliness of the soldier's death. He equates the brightness of the stolen helmet to the vivid poppy, and Euryalus's slender neck to the poppy's tired stalk, which droops and withers as it yields to the plow or heavy rain. The helmet's high plume, presumably scarlet, probably sparks the poppy comparison, underscoring its proliferation in the Northern and Central Italian countryside, and adding poignancy to the contrast between militarism and nature. Its red color is blood-like and aggressive, like death and parts of the Roman soldier's uniform. The passing plough that destroys these beautiful flowers proposes the cost of cultivation, or political progress as in the current Roman trajectory that destroys young men like Euryalus. Virgil evokes the significance of dress again when he enlists an image of the slain soldier's mother, whose shuttle and skein fall from her hands on hearing of her son's death. He will never wear the tunic she so lovingly weaves. With this micro-level item, a high-plumed helmet, which sculptor Jean-Baptiste Roman carves in marble (Figure 3.8), Virgil exposes a macro-level problem and dispenses a moral lesson: the terrible cost of Empire.

Figure 3.8: *Nisus and Euryalus*

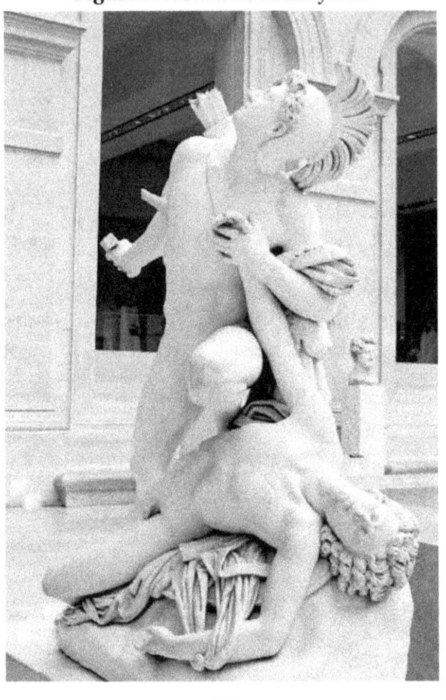

Jean-Baptiste Roman, 1827 (1792-1835); marble; 1.67 m x 1.4 m x 0.8 m; 65 ½ in. x 55 in. x 31 ¼ in; Acc no. LL 450; Louvre Museum; credit: © Marie-Lan Nguyen / Wikimedia Commons; http://imagencpd.aut.org/4DPict?file=20&rec=34.891&field=2 (accessed October 27, 2022).

The boy's sorry fate emphasizes the price of plunder as part of the cost of war along with the failings and sorrowful plight of humans, a constant Virgilian theme that gains amplification with the next example.

Camilla's Coveted Finery

In our second example of taking, we summon the warrior princess Camilla with her fatal sartorial desire and, again, see how Virgil uses attire to transmit meanings and acknowledge multilevel problems. Here, the finery so desired by Camilla is the catalyst for her death. Pledged to the goddess Diana and protected by Jupiter, Virgil bucks epic tradition and introduces her in a place of honor at the end of the catalog of warriors: "Divine Camilla," brave and beautiful with "unarmored breast and golden bow," a present from the goddess Diana, kills with aplomb and rides exultant with "her staunch handmaidens…

the Amazons of Thrace" (7.1115-1122).[61] Camilla and her Amazons, Larina and Tulla, wear painted gear and bear crescent shields while Tarpia wields a bronze studded axe like the one shown in Figure 3.9 in which she is being captured by her Phrygian cap.

Figure 3.9: *An Amazon with Battle-axe*

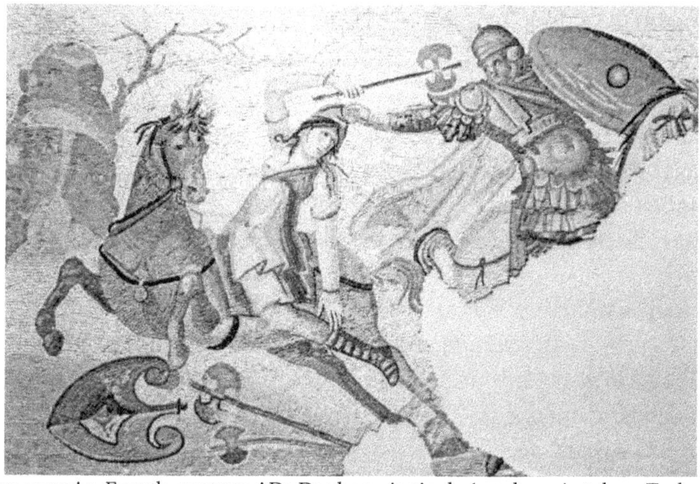

Roman mosaic; Fourth century AD; Daphne, Antioch (modern Antakya, Turkey); The Louvre; Credit to Jacques Mossot- Own work, CC BY-SA 4.0, https://commons.wikimedia.org/w/index.php?curid=37917418 (accessed September 19, 2022).

These are Italian women chosen by Camilla, and they join the war on the side of Turnus, the protagonist. Camilla spots Chloreus, the Phrygian soldier-priest, and is smitten by his splendidly showy clothes, so different from the make-shift or professional armor on the Latin soldiers, whom Virgil describes as having a variety of gear, including simple farming tools. [62] The exception are the patrician

---

[61] Davis Cleland and Lewellyn Jones eds., *Greek and Roman Dress*, 4 and 33, cite Amazon dress as eroticized after 440 BCE when we see a breast exposing *heteromaschalos* or *chitoniskos*, diminutive of chiton, knee-length or shorter, leaving one shoulder undone to expose the breast.

[62] Wolfgang Bruhn and Max Tilke, *A Pictorial History of Costume*, (London: Alpine Fine Arts Collection, 1991), 12, Phrygians are related to the Armenians from Asia Minor, agriculturalists known for their fine carpets and embroidery. Cleland, Davis and Lewellyn-Jones eds., *Greek and Roman Dress*, 57, write that according to Pliny the Elder

soldiers like Pallas and Turnus, who are handsomely clad, and with whom Camilla is familiar. The Trojans, however, are Easterners like the priest, and referred to as "[t]all men in strange costumes" (Aen.7.224) dressed in red and yellow with sleeves on their tunics and ribbons on their caps, looking more like women than men (Aen.9.855-857). At this time, Phrygian or Eastern clothing is generally richer in color, intricately patterned, and ornate than that of the West; hence, it is often described as effeminate. Indeed, there may have been little difference in the look of this priest, Chloreus, in his Eastern gear and Aeneas.[63]

The possibility of Camilla ever owning such richly decorated clothes is slim, as the Eastern fabrics available for the elite are too costly for a forest princess, and as a motherless child, she does not learn to spin or weave, so she cannot make anything like this for herself. Yet despite being raised in the forest by her exiled father and wearing only a tiger-skin as a child, Camilla is admired for her style, and sees her chance to enhance this by acquiring these exotic trappings.[64]

> By chance Chloreus, Mount Cybelus' votary,
> Once a priest, came shining from far off
> In Phrygian gear. He spurred a foaming mount
> In a saddle-cloth of hide with scales of bronze
> As thick as plumage, interlinked with gold.
> The man himself, splendid in rust and purple
> Out of the strange East, drew a Lycian bow
> To shoot Gortynian arrows: at his shoulder
> Golden was the bow and golden too
> The helmet of the seer, and tawny gold
> The broach that pinned his cloak as it belled out
> And snapped in wind, a chlamys a crocus-yellow.

---

embroidery was regarded by the Greeks and Romans as having been invented by the Phrygians.

[63] Mark Griffiths "What Does Aeneas Look Like" in Classical Philology Vol. 80, No. 4 , 309-319 Chicago UP, https://www.jstor.org/stable/i211930 (accessed January 10, 2023), raises the question as to how different this priest in his Eastern gear would have been from Aeneas, another Easterner? Given Virgil's description of the Trojan soldiers, probably not much.

[64] Michael C. J. Putnam, "Ganymede and Virgilian Ekphrasis." *The American Journal of Philology* 116:3 (1995): 419-440, 429, n.13. The Latin description of Chloreus' cloak as *femineo praedae et poliorum...armore* implies effeminacy, which Romulus' rebuke of Trojan clothing as red and yellow and beribboned also suggests (Aen.9.855).

Tunic and trousers, too, both Eastern style,
Were brilliant with embroidery (11.1045-1058).

This striking foreigner with a golden helmet and billowing yellow chlamys mesmerizes Camilla, who becomes blindly intent on tracking him. She fails to grasp the warning signal of the color yellow that, in Roman society, is appropriate for the wedding veil, but not for a war leader. His chlamys is also suspect. Worn by one who was a priest in Cybele and therefore a eunuch, it acknowledges "his improper role as war hero."[65] Blissfully unaware of these ominous overtones, Camilla shadows this brilliant figure swathed in exquisite trappings that goad her on to their possible attainment. Further lured by the glow of his animal-bronzed saddle-cloth, she anticipates ownership of this alluring finery. As Benjamin opines, "the most interesting thing about fashion is its extraordinary anticipations." These anticipations, however, blur Camilla's judgment. Dazzled by the idea of this finery for herself, either for adornment or trophy, she sees her chance, and wastes no time in seeking to satisfy her desire. She rides headlong into impending danger with a dark, dream-like consciousness to which fashion or finery adhere. Fearless of death, never doubting her ability to achieve her goal, and unimpeded by arguments of ethics, she is single-minded in her pursuit (11.1058-1066).[66]

Arruns, a Phrygian soldier, watches intently in the background and awaits his chance to kill this untamed huntress whose skills and courage shame regular soldiermen. Shrewdly, he seizes the moment, gives reign to his mount, lets his javelin fly, and prays for its accuracy. His prayers are answered. Superhuman power bestows the penetrating javelin to Camilla's unarmored breast, and drinks not the milk but the blood of the warrior-princess (11.1091-1096). Visions of darkness come to mind, another recurring Virgilian theme of how darkness adheres to the human condition.

Again, Virgil deploys dress to probe this darkness. He relentlessly questions the morality and loss in human life that cultural practices associated with the Empire accept and promote. Here, plunder becomes a reason to fight and win. Temptations of foreign exotica incite vanity, and the decision to kill comes easily; the outcome is tragic. In full circle, the fatal garments that provoke Camilla's death trigger that of their owner, who, like Euryalus, is spotted because of his brilliant attire and killed forthwith by an avenging soldier. The

---

[65] Bender, "De Habitu Vestis," 150.

[66] Benjamin, *Arcades Project*, 393

similarities of an admiring public, leadership, attraction to foreignness, courage, and the hunt and death entangle Camilla and Dido. Articles of attire, however, connect them even more deeply.

One interesting connection between the two Virgilian Queens comes with the use of animal skins. As noted, a tiger skin is Camilla's dress as a wild forest-child; and Dido is familiar with animal skins and their advantages as well. When the Sidonian princess first arrives in Carthage, she asks the ruling prince of North Africa, Iarbus, to sell her as much land as a bull's hide can cover. When the transaction is complete, however, the prince realizes he was tricked, for instead of a piece of land the size of a single bull's hide, the ingenious Dido has cut the skin in strips and pieced together an outline for the perimeter of an extensive city. Smitten Iarbus proposes but fails to win the lady's hand.

Moreover, other articles of dress tie Dido and Camilla together through equestrian prowess and the motif of the hunt. As a young horse-woman Camilla sports a golden hair broach reminiscent of Dido's golden broach on her gold and scarlet dress beneath the chlamys that she dons for the hunt that ends in her dubious marriage. The difference is Camilla's golden broach is a hair ornament, while Dido's pins to her dress. Also, both carry golden sheathed quivers, which evoke images of Diana, goddess of the hunt, Opis, her fleet huntress, as well as Venus and Ida, all of whom Virgil disguises as huntresses at some point in his poem. Using the hunt motif in which there is always a killing and always a victim, Virgil connects all of these women and unites what is going on in the poem through mythology.

Although Dido's fatal finery is a gift, while Camilla's is to be obtained by plunder, the deaths of both women link to items of dress. Virgil endorses Benjamin's premise that "all beautiful expressions are susceptible to more than one meaning,"[67] and deploys articles of dress to comment on the frailties of both leadership and life. The old French text, Roman d'Eneas, which originates from this epic, recalls the Latin and Greek derivation of the word gift as a dose of poison, and here the gift is "the luscious, amorous silk, which has replaced the scepter of governance, ...that draws Dido into a fateful love affair that marks the end of her ability to rule."[68] The "luscious amorous silk" is the poison, like the luxurious clothing that goads Camilla to ride fiercely on in her dream-like determination with no thought for safety. Although Camilla's death is not self-

---

[67] Benjamin, *Arcades Project*, 482.

[68] Jane Burns, *Sea of Silk: A Textile Geography of Women's Work in Medieval French Literature* (Philadelphia PEN: UP, 2009), 110.

inflicted, unlike Dido's, thoughts of attire supplant those of judgment and leadership. The indirect cause of Camilla's death parallels Dido's suicide when she addresses the resplendent clothes from Aeneas (4.898-900). In both cases, finery exposes frailty. Benjamin's judgment of fashion as the "provocation of death through the woman" fits here, as articles of dress emerge as instruments of destruction for both these Virgilian queens, exposing frailties in their lives and leadership skills that ultimately lead to their tragic ends.[69] Yet perhaps the most tragic death that is associated with attire awaits us in the third example of taking and final item for discussion.

Pallas's Sword-Belt

This dress item speaks loudly about the cost of war in lives lost, and besides plunder, questions the concept of heroism. The connotations that Virgil ascribes to taking or plunder are magnified in Turnus's actions, when after killing Pallas, he cannot resist taking the young prince's sword-belt, a cherished item of the boy, but acceptable spoils for the victor.

> He pressed with his heavy foot upon the dead
> And pulled away the massive weight of swordbelt
> Graven with pictured crime; that company,
> Aegyptus' sons, killed by Danaus' daughters,
> Young men murdered on one wedding night,
> Their nuptial beds blood-stained. Eurytus' son,
> Clonus, had chased the images in gold.
> Now Turnus gloried in it, in his winning.
> (10.694-703).

Here, we have a piece of dress heavily laden with rich historical imagery. The golden images engraved by Clonus, the son of Eurytus, adorning the sword-belt worn by Prince Pallas, are irresistible to Turnus, who triumphantly buckles it around himself as a trophy from his win. Here, as before most events in the *Aeneid*, Virgil forewarns us of impending doom in an oblique prophesy: "The minds of men are ignorant of fate, and of their future lot, unskilled to keep due measure when some triumph sets them high" (10.701-703). Virgil warns that Turnus's act of plunder will bring some future peril. Indeed, at the epic's end,

---

[69] Benjamin, *Arcades Project*, 63.

the sight of Pallas's sword-belt angers Aeneas so much that he subsequently reneges on his initial position of mercy toward Turnus and murders him.

Figure 3.10: *Aeneas defeats Turnus*

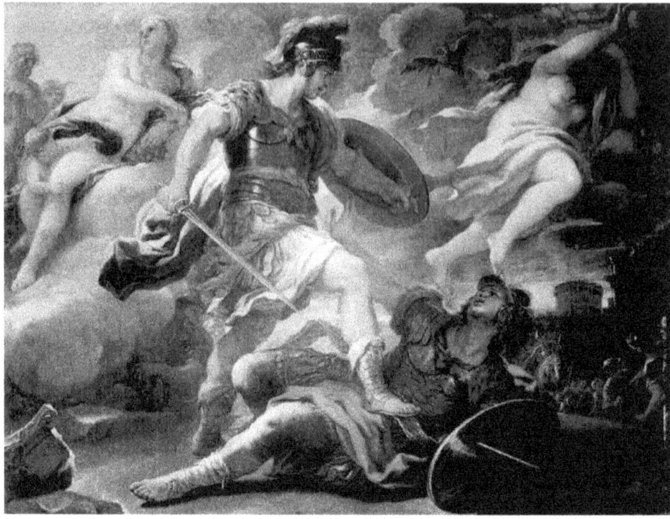

Luca Giordano, Italian (1634–1705); oil on canvas 176 x 236 cm; 69.2 x 92.9 in; Palazzo Corsini, Florence; https://commons.wikimedia.org/wiki/Template:PD-1996 (accessed June 28, 2022).

Prophetically, this belt depicts a scene of domestic violence, young husbands murdered on their wedding night, adding cruel irony to a perpetual Virgilian theme. A woman is involved here: Lavinia, Latinus's daughter, is promised to both Turnus and Aeneas; and for Turnus, this war is to win his bride, and this is to be his wedding night. Yet for Aeneas, Pallas's sword-belt reminds him of his failure to honor his promise to King Evander that his son would live. Killing Turnus becomes not an act of war but an emotional debt, a sacred obligation. As a direct consequence of seeing the swordbelt on Turnus, the Trojan hero and founder of the Roman race kills his worthy opponent in the act that ends the epic. (12.1081-1298). This is the final sartorial example of the syndrome of taking by plunder, and this closing scene of the epic derives from the ability of an article of dress to prompt memories that enrage enough to kill, driving home with a concluding thrust the now familiar Virgilian themes.

To illustrate the dark side of this wide-spread practice of plunder, Virgil employs pieces of armor that are etched with visible images, along with written

images of soldiers like Turnus, Euryalus, the Phrygian priest, and the warrior princess Camilla. We his readers, only imagine the three dimensionalities of these images, which supports Barthes's theory that written clothes are all of the imagination.[70] For our comprehension, Virgil plants "the crystal of the total event" in his analysis of the small individual image or dress item.[71] Euryalus's helmet, the soldier-priest's Eastern finery, and Pallas's sword-belt are crystals that reflect in multiple images the terrible cost of war and plead for peace. Virgil successfully employs this technique by polishing these written images to the degree that they reflect the personal histories and ideologies of their various owners. For example, he tells us about all the men who have been given, taken, or worn Euryalus's helmet and Pallas's swordbelt. The ideals they try to uphold, and the battles they try to fight. During the telling, all are dead but Turnus, and we have just discussed his fate. By using items of dress as his adopted ally, Virgil links cultural ideology with historical materialism to probe accepted practices; and all through words.

In conclusion, Virgil employs articles of attire with their social histories and cultural biographies to convey his intentions and drive his questions home. The questions are pertinent, even harsh, but because their vehicle of conveyance is gentle, commonly used for trivia, and not a tribunal, they are allowed to pass. Besides being literary adornments, these articles of attire speak with a cultural dialect that is understood by most who care to ponder their messages. In this reach for answers, dress emerges as a meaningful site of interaction for historical, mythological, and ideological information. It inflames memories that revisit past actions, igniting them into present realities that provoke future events. Virgil engages these memories held within a simple piece of cloth, leather, or metal to inspire deep passions and prompt heinous crimes. They are his narrative tools.

In examining the two broad themes (1) giving through the ritual of gifts, and (2) taking through the practice of plunder, Virgil precedes Benjamin when he "assemble[s] large scale constructions out of the smallest and most precisely cut components." Building a great empire, a large-scale construction, involves numerous small, meticulous, and widely accepted practices, precisely cut components, like those required to satisfy Zenia, and plunder. Yet these seemingly insignificant practices link personal responsibility to the authority of empire, and individual actions to large events. Using meaning-laden

---

[70] Barthes, *Language of Fashion*, 76.

[71] Benjamin, *Arcades Project*, 460-461.

presents for Dido from the legendary Helen and royal relics from Troy, along with Dido's gifts to Aeneas, in particular the sparkling Sidonian cloaks that find their afterlife as a shroud on Pallas's pyre, and the deeply etched sword-belt that ultimately ends the epic, Virgil depicts the hopeless entangling of events of person and state as he negotiates and questions historical and cultural customs and forms. These dress items represent the precise personal social processes that custom requires, but they simultaneously situate these processes within a large public sphere, where the cost may be death itself, as we see with Dido, Camilla, Pallas, and Turnus.[72]

Virgil endows these vestimentary vehicles with attributes more often associated with commodities or things for barter, which rest comfortably in the heart of exchange theory. Yet his exchanges question and fulfill cultural traditions, and personal desires that propel the plot to its final end. These highly illuminated and well-circulated items of attire portray the tensions and ambiguities associated with identity and empire building on an epic level and herald the importance of written dress in the ancient world.

Bibliography

Aeneid, Virgil. Trans. Robert Fitzgerald. New York: Random House, 1990.

Alighieri, Dante. *The Inferno*. New York: Random House, 2010.

Appadurai, Arjun. Introduction: "Commodities and the Politics of Value." In *The Social Life of Things*, 3-63. Ed. Arjun Appadurai. Cambridge: Cambridge UP, 1988.

Augustine. City of God. Trans. Henry Bettenson. London: Penguin Books, 1972 (1467).

Barchiesi, Alessandro. "Virgilian Narrative: Ecphrasis." In *The Cambridge Companion*, 271-282. Ed. Charles Martindale, Cambridge U. K.: Cambridge UP, 1997.

Barthes, Roland. *The Language of Fashion*. Trans. Andy Stafford. Ed. Andy Stafford and Michael Carter. Oxford: Berg, 2006.

Bartlett, Djurdja. Introduction. In *Fashion and Politics*, 1-17. Ed. Djurdia Bartlett. New Haven and London: Yale UP, 2019.

Batten, Alicia J. "Clothing and Adornment," *Biblical Theology Bulletin: A Journal of Bible and Theology* 40:3 (2010).

Bender, Henry. "De Habitu Vestis: Clothing in the Aeneid." In *The World of Roman Costume*, 146-152. Eds. Judith L. Sebesta and Larissa Bonfante. Madison, Wis: University of Wisconsin Press, 1994.

---

[72] Benjamin, *Arcades Project*, 460-461.

Benjamin, Walter. *Arcades Project.* Trans. Howard Eiland and Kevin McLaughlin. Eds. Rolf Tiedemann. Cambridge, MA: Harvard UP, 2002.

Boulnois, Luce. *Silk Road.* Trans. Helen Loveday. Hong Kong: Odyssey Books and Guides, 2001.

Brennan, T. Corey. "Tertullian's De Pallio and Roman Dress in North Africa." *In Roman Dress and the Fabrics of Roman Culture,* 258-270. Eds. Jonathan Edmondson and Alison Keith. Toronto: UP, 2008.

Bruhn, Wolfgang, and Max Tilke. *A Pictorial History of Costume.* London: Alpine Fine Arts Collection, 1991.

Burns, Jane. *Sea of Silk: A Textile Geography of Women's Work in Medieval French Literature.* Philadelphia: UP, 2009.

Carins, Douglas L. "The Meaning of the Veil in Ancient Greek Culture." In *Women's Dress in the Ancient Greek World,* 73-93. Ed. Lloyd Llewellyn Jones. London: The Classical Press of Wales, 2002.

Chaucer, Geoffrey. "The House of Fame." In *The Concise Oxford Companion to English Literature.* Eds. Margaret Drabble, Jenny Stringer and Daniel Hahn. Oxford: UP, 2007.

Clader, Linda Lee. *Helen: The Evolution from Divine to Heroic in Greek Epic Tradition.* Leiden, the Netherlands: E. J. Brill, 1976.

Clausen, Wendell. *Virgil's Aeneid: Decorum, Allusion, and Ideology.* Leipzig: K. G. Saur München, 2002.

Cleland, Liza, Glenys Davis and Lloyd Lewellyn-Jones. Eds. *Greek and Roman Dress from A-Z.* London and New York: Routledge, 2007.

Cleland, Liza, Mary Harlow and Lloyd Llewellyn-Jones, Eds. *The Clothed Body in the Ancient World.* Oxford: Oxbow, 2005.

Croom, Alexandra T. *Roman Clothing and Fashion.* Stroud, Gloucestershire: Tempus, 2002.

Cook, Richard. *Helen and Priam at the Scaen Gate.*1808. Digital image file no.16286; Source File no. FPa75; Folger Shakespeare Library. https://commons.wikimedia.org/wiki/Template:PD-1996. Accessed January 10, 2023.

Davies, Glenys, "What Made the Roman Toga *virilis*?" In *The Clothed Body in the Ancient World,* 119-130.

Delgado, Henry Navarro. "Fashion's Potential to Influence Politics and Culture." CNN Style. 2018. https://www.cnn.com/style/article/fashion-influence-politics-and-culture/index.html /. Accessed January 28, 2023.

Douglas, Mary, and Baron Isherwood. *The World of Goods: Toward and Anthropology of Consumption.* New York: Basic, 1979.

Durkheim, Emile. *The Elementary Forms of Religious Life.* Trans. Carol Cosman. New York: Oxford UP, 2001.

Edmondson, Jonathan, and Allison Keith. Eds. *Roman Dress and the Fabrics of Roman Culture.* Toronto: UP, 2008.

Edmondson, Jonathan. "Public Dress and Social Control in Late Republican and Early Imperial Rome." In *Roman Dress and the Fabrics of Roman Culture,* 21-46.

Edwards, Douglas R. "The Social, Religious, and Political Aspects of Costume in Josephus." In *The World of Roman Costume,* 153-159.

Fanfani, Giovanni, Mary Harlow, and Mary Louise Nosch, Eds. *Spinning Fates and The Song of the Loom: The Use of Textiles, Clothing and Cloth Production as Metaphor, Symbol and Narrative Device in Greek and Latin Literature, Textile History.* Oxford: Oxbow, 2016.

Ferrari, Luca. *Venus Prevents her Son Aeneas from Killing Helen of Troy* c.1650 acc. no.1460; Art Gallery of South Australia; https://en.wikipedia.org/wiki/en :LibraryofCongress. Accessed January 18, 2023.

Gibbon, Edward. Ed. *The History of the Decline and Fall of the Roman Empire.* Chapter 27. London: Strahan and Cadell, 1776-1789.

Giordano, Luca. *Aeneas Defeats Turnus* (1634–1705). Palazzo Corsini, Florence; https://commons.wikimedia.org/wiki/Template:PD-1996. Accessed June 28, 2022.

Goffman, Erving. *Interaction Ritual.* New York: Doubleday, 1967.

Goffman, Erving. *The Presentation of Self in Everyday Life.* Garden City, New York: Doubleday, 1959.

Goffman, Erving. "The Nature of Deference and Demeanor." *American Anthropologist* 58:3 (1956): 475-499.

Griffiths, Mark. "What Does Aeneas Look Like." In *Classical Philology* Vol. 80, No. 4, 309-319. Chicago UP. https://www.jstor.org/stable/i211930. Accessed January 27, 2023.

Guyer, Jane. "Personal and Real Law." In Marcel Mauss, *The Gift: Expanded Edition,* 122. Selected, Annot. and Trans. Jane I. Guyer. Foreword Bill Maurer. Chicago: U. P., 2016.

Hanson, Victor Davis. "The Strange Morality of the Bay-Area Billionaire Left." American Greatness. 2022. https://amgreatness.com/2022/11/20/the-strange-morality-of-the-bay-area-billionaire-left/. Accessed January 28, 2023.

Hardie, Philip R. *Vergil's Aeneid: Cosmos and Imperium.* Oxford: UP, 1986.

Harlow, Mary. Ed. *A Cultural History of Dress and Fashion, vol. 1 Antiquity.* London: Bloomsbury Academic, 2016.

Harlow, Mary. "Literary Representations." In *Cultural History of Dress and Fashion, vol. 1 Antiquity 1-17.*

Harlow, Mary. "Dress in the Historia Augusta: The Role of Dress in Historical Narrative." In *The Clothed Body in the Ancient World,* 142-153.

Iliad. Homer. Trans. Robert Fitzgerald. Intro. Andrew Ford. New York: Farrar, Straus and Giroux. 1974, 2004.

Jashemski. Wilhelmina Feemster, Frederick G. Meyer and Massimo Ricciardi. "Plants: Evidence from Wall Paintings, Mosaics, Sculpture, Plant Remains,

Graffiti, Inscriptions and Ancient Authors." In *The Natural History of Pompeii, Vol.1.* 1st Ed. 80-180. Ed. Wilhelmina Feemster. Cambridge: UP, 2002.

Jenkins, David. "The Ambiguity of Greek Textiles." in *Arethusa* 18.2 (1985): 109-132.

Johnson W. Ralph. *Darkness Visible: A Study of Vergil's Aeneid.* Berkeley: UP, 1976.

Kim, Jung Hoon. *The Significance of Clothing Imagery.* London: T and T Clark, 2004.

Koortbojian, Michael. "Costumes and their Symbolism at Rome." In *Roman Dress and the Fabrics of Roman Culture*, 81-94.

La Follette, Laetitia, "The Costume of the Roman Bride." In *The World of Roman Costume* 54-64. Eds. Judith Lynn Sebesta and Larissa Bonfante. Madison, Wisconsin: Wisconsin U.P., 1994.

Lewellyn-Jones, Lloyd. Ed. *Women's Dress in the Ancient Greek World.* Swansea: Classical Press of Wales, 2002.

Marlowe, Christopher. *Dido, Queen of Carthage.* New York: Random House, 1983.

Matheson, Linda. "Imperial Material: Modern Western Fashion Theory and a Seventeenth-Century Eastern Empire." *Dress, the Journal of the Costume Society of America* 37:1 (Oct, 2011): 57-82.

Matheson, Linda. "Virgil's Aeneid." In *Divinely Attired,* 151-193. Davis, University of California, 2012.

Martindale, Charles. Ed. *The Cambridge Companion to Virgil.* Cambridge: UP, 1997.

Martindale, Charles. "Introduction: The Classic of all Europe." In *The Cambridge Companion to Virgil*, 1-19.

Marx, Karl. *The Social and Political Thought of Karl Marx.* Cambridge: Cambridge UP, 1970.

Maurer, Bill. "Foreword." In *The Gift: Expanded Edition.* Marcel Mauss. Selected, Annotated and Trans. by Jane I. Guyer. Chicago: UP, 2016, xv.

Mauss, Marcel. *The Gift: Expanded Edition.* Selected, Annotated and Trans. Jane I. Guyer. Foreword Bill Maurer. Chicago: UP, 2016.

Mauss, Marcel. *The Gift.* Trans. Ian Cunnison. Intro. E. E. Evans-Pritchard. New York: Norton, 1967.

McCracken, Grant. *Culture and Consumption: New Approaches to the Symbolic Character of Consumer Goods and Activities.* Bloomington: Indiana UP, 1988.

Miettinen, Reijo. "Artifact Mediation in Dewey and in Cultural-Historical Activity Theory." *Mind, Culture, and Activity* 8:4 (2001): 297-308.

Murphy, Robert Francis. *Social Distance and the Veil.* London: Berg, 1999.

Nussbaum, Martha. "Veiled Threats" *The New York Times.* Opinionator. July 11, 2010. Accessed November 28, 2023.

Odyssey. Homer. Trans. Stanley Lombardo. Cambridge: Hackett, 2000.

Odyssey. Homer. Trans. Robert Fitzgerald. New York: Random, 1990.

Oliver, Richard and Allen Marcus Lyne. *Words and the Poet: Characteristic Techniques of Style in Vergil's Aeneid.* Oxford: UP, 1989.

Olsen, Kelly. *Dress and the Roman Women: Self-Presentation and Society.* London and New York: Routledge, 2007.

Ovid. *Heroides in Heroides and Amores.* Ed. Grant Showerman. London: William Heinemann, 1931.

Ovid. *Metamorphoses.* Ed. and Trans. Frank Justus Miller. 3rd Edn. Cambridge, Mass.: Harvard UP, 1984.

Peirce, Charles S. *Philosophical Writings of Peirce.* New York: Dover, 1955.

Peirce, Charles S. "Scientific Metaphysics." In *Collected Papers of Charles Sanders Peirce,* Vol.6, 272-77. Eds. Charles Hartshorne and Paul Weiss. Cambridge, MA: Harvard UP, 1935.

Petrie, Sir William Matthews Flinders. "Egypt." In *the Encyclopedia Britannica,* Vol 15, 11th Ed. 279. Cambridge: UP, 1911.

Putnam, Michael C. J. "Ganymede and Virgilian Ekphrasis." *The American Journal of Philology* 116:3 (1995): 419-440.

Reinhold, Meyer. *History of Purple as a Status Symbol in Antiquity.* Bruxelles: Latomus Revue d' Etudes Latines, 1970.

Roman, Jean-Baptiste. *Nisus and Euryalus.* 1827. Acc no. LL 450; Louvre Museum; credit: © Marie-Lan Nguyen / Wikimedia Commons; http://imagencpd.aut.org/4DPict?file=20&rec=34.891&field=2. Accessed October 27, 2022.

Sacchi, Andrea. *Death of Dido.* Early seventeenth-century. Beaux-Art de Caen; https://commons.wikimedia.org/wiki/Template:PD-1996. Accessed January 25, 2023.

Scott, Wallach J. *The Politics of the Veil.* Princeton, NJ: Princeton UP, 2007.

Sebesta, Judith Lynn. "Visions of Gleaming Textiles and a Clay Core: Greek Women and Pandora." In *Women's Dress in the Ancient Greek World,* 125-142.

Sebesta, Judith Lynn, and Larissa Bonfante, Eds. *The World of Roman Costume.* Madison, Wisconsin: Wisconsin UP, 1994.

Sebesta, Judith Lynn. "Symbolism in the Costume of Roman Women." In *The World of Roman Costume,* 46-53.

Sebesta, Judith Lynn. "Tunica Ralla, Tunica Spissa: The Colors and Textiles of Roman Costume." In *The World of Roman Costume,* 65-76.

Shakespeare, William. "Troilus and Cressida" In *The Arden Shakespeare,* 261-324. Ed. Kenneth Palmer. London: Methuen, 1982.

Simmel, Georg. "Fashion." *International Quarterly* 10:1(1990): 130-155.

Snyder, Jane. "The Web of Song: Weaving Imagery in Homer and the Lyric Poets." *The Classical Journal* 76: 3 (1981): 192-198.

Spencer, Edmund. *The Faerie Queene.* New York: Penguin Classics, 1979.

Spencer, Herbert. "Badges and Costumes." In *The Principles of Sociology.* New York: Appleton, 1924.

Stallaert, Joseph. *The Death of Dido.* 1872. Royal Museums of Fine Arts of Belgium, Brussels; https://commons.wikimedia.org/wiki/Template:PD-1996. Accessed January 25, 2023.

Tiepolo. Giovanni Battista. *Venus Appears to Aeneas on the Shores of Carthage.* 1757. Credit: Web Gallery of Art https://commons.wikimedia.org/wiki/Template:PD-1996. Accessed January 15, 2023.

Tischbein, Johann Heinrich. *Aeneas before Dido.* 1773. https://datenbank.museum-kassel.de/28523; https://commons.wikimedia.org/wiki/Template:PD-1996. Accessed January 16, 2023.

Tortora, Phyllis G. and Keith Eubank. *Survey of Historic Costume: A History of Western Dress.* Third Ed. New York: Fairchild, 2001.

Tulloch, Carol. "T-Shirt Matters." In *Fashion Knowledge: Theories, Methods, Practices and Politics,* 113-135. Bristol, Chicago: Intellect, 2022.

Verkolye, Nicolas. *Dido and Aeneas.* Early eighteenth-century. Acc no. 71. PA.66; Source: The J. Paul Getty Museum, Los Angeles; https://commons.wikimedia.org/wiki/Template:PD-1996. Accessed January 18, 2023.

Vergil's Aeneid, A Dual Language Edition. Trans and Ed. Joshua W. D. Smith. Bolton, On: Amazon.ca manufacturer, 2017.

Vinken, Barbara. "Fashion, an Oriental Tyranny in the Heart of the West." In *Fashion and Politics,* 61-72. Yale UP, 2019.

Virgil: *The Aeneid.* Trans. A. S. Kline, 2002, PIT Poetry in Translation. www.tonykline.co.uk. Accessed November 15, 2022.

Vogelzang, Mary and W. J. van Bekkum. "Meaning and Symbolism of Clothing in Ancient Near Eastern Texts." In *Scripta Signa Vocis,* 265-284. Ed. H. L. J. Vanstiphout. Groningren: E. Forsten,1986.

Weiss, Hans Van. "Trailing Tunics and Sheepskin Coats: Dress and Status in Early Greece." In *The Clothed Body in the Ancient World,* 44-51.

Wilcox, Turner. *The Mode in Costume.* New York: Scribner's Sons, 1958 [1942].

Wilson, Elizabeth. *Unfolding the Past.* London: Bloomsbury, 2022.

Your Dictionary: https://www.yourdictionary.com/jasper; From *American Heritage Dictionary of the English Language,* 5th ed. and *Wiktionary.* Accessed November 18, 2022.

Chapter 4

Historical Costume: Acknowledging the Distinctiveness Between the Centuries and Epochs

Damayanthie Eluwawalage
Delaware State University

Abstract: In any historical study, literary texts should be interpreted within the appropriate historical context, especially when analyzing costumes. The differences between centuries are significantly varied in the context of human deportment, customs, traditions, and attitudes. Manners and deportment are constantly transformed by changing society. The differences in clothing styles between the centuries are significant. Cutting and construction techniques also varied considerably from century to century as each era produced its own unique decorations and silhouettes. Clothes represent an art form ascending out of a particular period and environment. Differences in fashion theories also reflect different eras, and the study will explore those pertinent fashion theories between the fifteenth to nineteenth centuries. Also, the psychological, sociological, and gender aspects of costume will be discussed in theoretical contexts.

Keywords: Theory, Philosophy, Deportment, Techniques, Class, Gender, Etiquette, Fashion, Zeitgeist, Vestimentary Codes

***

> "If Roman Life is not to become lost in anachronisms or petrified in abstraction, we must study it within a strictly defined period."[1]

---

[1] Jerome Carcopino, *Daily Life in Ancient Rome* (London: Penguin Books, 1941), 9. Will Durant, *The Story of Philosophy* (London: Ernest Benn, 1927).

In any historical study, literary texts should be interpreted within the appropriate historical and theoretical context, as distinguished by characteristics common to any given era, period, or movement, especially analyzing and examining costumes and clothing.[2] Specifically, in applying, interpreting, and selecting theories, it must be developed in the era of investigation for several reasons, which will be briefly, interdisciplinarily, and collectively discussed throughout the chapter. With reference to historical criticism or literary criticism in the light of historical evidence or based on the context in which a work was written, including facts about the author's life and the historical and social circumstances of the time.[3] The above-mentioned phenomenon is relevant and applicable to every aspect of any society and life. For example, in his introduction to Geoffrey Chaucer's *Canterbury Tales*[4], Gordon Hall Gerould wrote, "Poets born on the edge of a new era stand in peculiar danger of being misunderstood and depreciated by the generations that follow. Since time never stands still, and one age is forever melting into the next, any poet has to take a rather desperate chance of appealing to readers beyond his own day. There is always the possibility, to be sure, that he may be more highly esteemed than by his contemporaries—a faint hope that has buoyed up many who were destined to drown in the waters of oblivion— but this does not often happen. The inevitable revaluation usually marks the poet down to a lower figure. Sometimes, he has to wait a few centuries before he is understood and appreciated again."[5] Also, in concurrence with the above, as Young examines in her *Recurring Cycles of Fashion 1760-1937,* the perpetual and varied nature of trend changes in clothing and fashion is a phenomenon distinctly noticeable throughout history in any given time and place.[6]

In the framework of the body of written works of a language, period, or culture, according to Fleming, historical context is an important part of life and literature, and without it, memories, stories, and characters have less meaning. In the

---

[2] Damayanthie Eluwawalage, "Dress Theory: Exploring Critical Issues" in *Trending Now,* eds. Laura Petican, Mariam Esseghaier, Angela Nurse,Damayanthie Eluwawalage, (London: Inter-disciplinary Press, 2013) ISBN: 978-1-84888-211-9, File type: eBook, 103-113.

[3] *Encyclopedia Britannica,* https://www.britannica.com/art/historical-criticism-literary-criticism. (accessed February 13, 2014).

[4] *The Canterbury Tales* is a collection of twenty-four stories that runs to over 17,000 lines written in Middle English by Geoffrey Chaucer between 1387 and 1400.

[5] Geoffrey Chaucer, *Canterbury Tales* (New York: Garden City Publishing Company, 1934), v.

[6] Agnes Brooks Young, *Recurring Cycles of Fashion 1760-1937* (New York & London: Harper & Brothers Publishers, 1937).

context of the principle hypothesis of this chapter,[7] historical context deals with the details that surround an occurrence and refers to the social, religious, economic, gender, and political conditions that existed during a certain era, time, and place. Fundamentally, it's all the details of the time and place in which a situation occurs, and those details are what enable us to interpret and analyze works or events of the past, or even the future, rather than merely judge them by contemporary standards. In literature and theory, a strong understanding of the historical context behind a work's creation can provide us with a better understanding of and appreciation for the narrative. In analyzing historical events, context can help us understand what motivates people to behave as they did, as historical context is important when interpreting behavior. For example, costume, fashion, attire, and dress in general and appearance in particular. Also, context is what gives meaning to the details. It's important, however, not to confuse context with cause. Cause is the action that creates an outcome; context is the environment in which that action and outcome occur.[8]

In accordance with the above, as Gerould wrote about the essence of Geoffrey Chaucer's time or the Age of Chaucer, the fourteenth century: "Chaucer had perfected from the speech of educated folk in London at his time a poetical instrument as flexible and melodious, as capable of expressing a wide range of feelings and ideas, as any English author has had at his command. But the speech of London changed very rapidly after his death in 1400. A century later the language was on the verge of becoming what we call modern English, and in fifty years more it was the native tongue of Spenser and Shakespeare. At the same time the ideas of men, together with the political and social fabric in which they found expression, changed with equal rapidity. Medieval England became Tudor England. Chaucer's language had by this time become archaic, as hard to understand as it is in the twentieth century, or indeed harder, since we have better editions with the notes and glossaries that scholars have industriously compiled. The codes according to which he thought and felt and acted had become old-fashioned, too, though not so remote as they are to us…"[9]

---

[7] - in any historical study literary texts should be interpreted within the appropriate historical and theoretical context -

[8] Grace Fleming, "The Importance of Historic Context in Analysis and Interpretation." *ThoughtCo.* https://www.thoughtco.com/what-is-historical-context-1857069 (accessed February 23, 2023).

[9] Geoffrey Chaucer, Canterbury Tales (New York: Garden City Publishing Company, 1934), v-vi.

In like manner, the law of change was not less operative in antiquity. During the Roman Empire for instance, it was a commonplace of Roman rhetoric to contrast the rude simplicity of the republic with the luxury and refinement of imperial times and to recall that Manius Curius Dentatus[10] - according to Decimus Junius Juvenalis, a Roman poet - "would cook humble Greens, picked in the garden, on his modest hearth, now Every squalid ditch-digger in the chain-gang would refuse it, While reminiscing about the tripe he ate in some steaming diner" There is no common measure, whether of food or house or furniture, between ages so different. [11] In concurring with the above, in his Daily Life in Ancient Rome, Jerome Carcopino states, "Nothing changes more rapidly than human customs. Apart from the recent scientific discoveries which have turned the world of today upside down - steam, electricity, railways, motor-cars, and aeroplanes — it is clear that even in times of greater stability and less highly developed technique the elementary forms of everyday life were subject to unceasing change. Coffee, tobacco, and champagne were not introduced into Europe until the seventeenth century; potatoes were first eaten toward the end of the eighteenth; the banana became a feature of our dessert at the beginning of the twentieth..."[12]

In analyzing the concept of historical occurrences should be clarified and understood within the appropriate historical framework, in gender context, as Broby-Johansen explains, "throughout the history of our civilization, it has been the task of women, albeit assisted on occasions by men, to establish and maintain the home as the vital center of family life. Men can establish a state, but what state can create a home atmosphere for its children? There are many things which will be treated with greater care and respect when a world exists in which women's power and influence is equal to that of men. When this time comes, the history of dress will have reached the end of an epoch and a new era will commence. No longer will dress and mode of dress be a sign of class and social standing or a method of disguise."[13]

Most importantly, the differences between centuries are significantly varied in the context of human deportment, customs, traditions, and attitudes.[14] In

---

[10] Roman General, conqueror of the Samnites and victor against Pyrrhus, King of Epirus

[11] Decimus Junius Juvenalis, *An Invitation to Dinner, The Food* (The Satires, Satire XI), 78-79.

[12] Jerome Carcopino, *Daily Life in Ancient Rome* (London: Penguin Books, 1941), 9.

[13] Rudolph Broby-Johansen, *Body and Clothes* (London: Faber and Faber Limited, 1968), 234.

[14] Joan Wildeblood, *The Polite World: A Guide to English Manners and Deportment* (London: Davis Poynter Ltd, 1965).

fact, the pursuit of etiquette has been a societal concern for centuries.[15] Manners and deportment are constantly transformed by changing society. Therefore, these social behaviors should not be regarded merely as details of little consequence; they are an expression of a particular era as much as any other outward manifestation. Thus, according to Roland Barthes, "When we examine how clothes define an individual, we must also set the man or woman within the context of their place and time," as the differences in clothing styles between the centuries are significant.[16] Cutting and construction techniques also varied considerably from century to century as each era produced its own unique decorations and silhouettes.[17] Clothes represent an art form ascending out of a particular period and environment. According to Francois Boucher, costume and, its application and meaning, have varied with each period. [18]

It is imperative to note that this idea can be precisely applicable to the decorative version of raiment, "fashion." According to Sapir, fashion is emphatically a historical concept. A specific fashion is utterly unintelligible if lifted out of its place in a sequence of forms. It is exceedingly dangerous to rationalize or in any other way psychologize a particular fashion on the basis of general principles which might be considered applicable to the class of forms of which it seems to be an example. It is utterly vain, for instance, to explain particular forms of dress or types of cosmetics or methods of wearing hair without a preliminary historical critique. Bare legs among modern women in summer do not psychologically or historically create at all the same fashion as bare legs and bare feet among primitives living in the tropics. The importance of understanding fashion historically should be obvious enough when it is recognized that the very essence of fashion is that it be valued as a variation in an understood sequence, as a departure from the immediately preceding mode.[19]

In conjunction with the above, Carlyle states that "the primary purpose of clothes was not warmth or decency, but ornament. The first spiritual want of a

---

[15] Joseph Dent. *Australian Etiquette: Rules and Usage of the Best Society* (London: D. E. McConnell, 1980).

[16] Anne Hollander, *Sex and Suits* (New York: Alfred A. Knoff, 1995).

[17] Gordon Wills & David Midgley, *Fashion Marketing: An Anthology of View Points and Perspectives* (London: Allen and Unwin Ltd, 1973), 12.

[18] François Boucher, *A History of Costume in the West* (London: Thames and Hudson, 1966), 5-6.

[19] Edward Sapir, 931 "Fashion" in *Encyclopedia of the Social Sciences VI* (New York: Macmillan, 1931), 141-142.

barbarous[20] man is Decoration. The Aboriginal Savage, for instance, "warmth he found in the toils of the chase; or amid dried leaves in his hollow tree, in his bark shed, or natural grotto, but for Decoration he must have Clothes, also tattooing and painting even prior to Clothes."[21] Most importantly, the above-mentioned notion is unique to a particular era in history, and not necessarily applicable to the subsequent or different centuries. Also, in the context of fashion, as civilization advanced, a style of dress gradually evolved, entirely different from the previous style.[22]

In another conceptual view of class-related theories, clothing and its ornamental version- fashion - is a product of class distinction. Fashion does not exist in tribal and classless societies.[23] The concept of class as a collection of individuals sharing similar economic and societal circumstances often reflected changes in the structure of Western European societies, especially after the industrial and political revolutions of the late Eighteenth century. Differences in fashion theories also reflect different eras. For example, nineteenth-century theorists, such as Veblen and Simmel, regarded differentiation and stratification as essential pre-conditions of fashion, while the twentieth-century theorist, Herbert Blumer, regards fashion as an expression of collective behavior, that is, the fashion mechanism appears not in response to a need for class differentiation and class emulation, but in response to a wish to be in fashion.[24]

In understanding existing theories in the fundamental premise of this chapter,[25] the theories of psychology and the theories of sociology in the context of costume, for instance, is intricate and is vividly discussed by econo-

---

[20] **Barbarous**: Extremely cruel or unpleasant, or failing to reach acceptable social standards (*Cambridge Dictionary*)

Barbarians: The Greeks called the native peoples of Europe outside their borders "barbarians." Today, most people use the term to mean someone or something coarse, uncultured, even crudely violent. They use the term loosely, as a pejorative for all that does not conform to some idea of what it means to be civilized. (Ancient Europe 8000 B.C.--A.D. 1000. (*Encyclopedia of the Barbarian world*, 3.)

[21] Thomas Carlyle, *Sartor resartus*, Archibold MacMechan, ed. (Boston and London: Ginn & Co., 1896), 33-34.

[22] Carl Kohler, *A History of Costume* (New York: Dover Publications, 1963), 67.

[23] George Simmel, "Fashion" in *American Journal of Sociology*, LX11 (1957), 541.

24 Herbert Blumer, "Fashion: From Class Differentiation to Collective Selection" in *The Sociological Quarterly*, 1969, Vol. 10), 275-291.

[25] - any historical study literary texts should be interpreted within the appropriate historical and theoretical context -

sociological theorists such as Thorstein Veblen and Georg Simmel. Veblen's Leisure Theory addresses modes of conduct, especially those of the nineteenth century. Veblen's theory of conspicuous consumption explains the fashion follower's motivation. His theory of economic consumption is based on the idea that people choose their clothing primarily to indicate their status to others. In the Theory of the Leisure Class, Veblen proposes "The valuation of persons in respect of worth" [26] which defines who is to be regarded as inferior and who is superior. He explains this difference in terms of employment, that is, the distinction between exploitation and drudgery. Employment, which is classified as exploit, is deemed honorable, worthy, and noble[27] whereas those tasks which actually involve work are deemed unworthy, debasing, and ignoble.[28] Therefore, Veblen bases his Leisure Theory on the emergence of the distinction between exploitative work and ordinary productive work and its application to the organization of the economic order. In Veblen's time, exploitative work brought financial success, enabling property ownership to be a conspicuous indicator of achieved status and entitlement.

A consequence of exploitative work was the delegation of tasks to those one employs. This then enables leisure time for those in control. The term leisure, for Veblen, means the "non-productive consumption of time."[29] But he also points out that "Conspicuous leisure wastes potential production and generates resistance to economic or social change. Conspicuous leisure is reflected in conspicuous consumption." Conspicuous consumption occurs when members of that society spend money on leisure and the appropriate clothing and services for leisure activities. This skews production to meet the demand for luxury goods and services. At the same time, the leisure class imposes guidelines, i.e., the way of dressing, for the lesser-classes. Dress and fashion, therefore, demonstrated both conspicuously and vicariously that the wearer was not only wealthy, but also was a member of the leisure-class.[30]

In the early twentieth century, in his *Fashion Simulation theory*, Simmel outlines the role of fashion in nineteenth-century societies, where social structure had distinct classes. Conclusively, the Pre-Twentieth century phenomenon, dress as an expression of the pecuniary culture, the trickle-down

---

[26] Thorstein Veblen, *The Theory of the Leisure Class* (London: Unwin Books, London), 34.

[27] Veblen, *The Theory of the Leisure Class*, 15.

[28] Veblen, *The Theory of the Leisure Class*, 15.

[29] Veblen, *The Theory of the Leisure Class*, 43.

[30] Veblen, *The Theory of the Leisure Class*, 68-101.

effect of consumption patterns from Leisure classes to the working classes is hardly applicable to the Post-Twentieth century societies, instead gradually, the trickle-up effect originated. Simmel's theory, too, advocates a trickle-down process of fashion, whereby styles that were first created and exhibited by the upper-class, were later adopted by the middle-class and lower-classes. According to Simmel, fashion is a form of imitation. Fashion is also an indication of internal social cohesion as people dress similarly to identify with each other. Fashion thus differentiates one social stratum from another. However, according to Simmel, this is an ever-changing process. Each time the elite initiate a fashion, and the masses imitate it in an effort to obliterate the distinction of class, the elite then abandons that style for an even newer mode to re-establish class distinction. This process also quickens with the increase of wealth. Fashion is, therefore, according to Simmel, an initiation of class distinction that does not exist in tribal or classless societies.[31]

In accordance with the chapter objective, every historical era has its own unique sociological, psychological, economic, political, and gender-related characteristics. Similarly, fashion and clothing are explicitly constitutive of historical epochs or periods.[32] Fashion, according to Nystrom, is nothing more or less than the prevailing style at any given time.[33] In line with the above, Horn states that it is a manifestation of collective behavior and, as such, represents the popular, accepted, general, and dominant style at any given time.[34]

Theoretically, fashion is a culturally and customarily endorsed form of non-verbal communication and expression in a particular material or non-material phenomenon, which is perceivable at any given era and mutates over time within a collective group or society. Also, as Bigelow examines, clothes — fashion's body coverings — are the wearable, sculptural art forms which individuals use to identify themselves as creatures of a specific period. In addition, individual selection of styles makes the wearer, in part, a creator. By their very selection, a person retains individuality and personality. By the same selectiveness, an individual maintains group and time identity. By combining

---

[31] George Simmel, "Fashion" in *American Journal of Sociology,* LX11 (1957), 541-558.
[32] Malcolm Barnard. "Fashion Theory: A Reader," in *Costume and Fashion* (London, New York: 2007), 37.
[33] Paul Henry Nystrom, *Economics of Fashion* (Chicago: The University of Chicago Press, 1928).
[34] Marilyn Horn, *The second skin* (Boston: Houghton Mifflin, 1968).

personal selection and creativity, the modes and manners of individual life-styles and period styles can be traced.[35]

In conjunction with the main objective of this chapter,[36] in bygone times, raiment was a form of imitation and, therefore, of social equalization. However, as societies changed over the centuries, an emergence of parallel theories was also evidenced. Most importantly, those theories are varied in accordance with the historical eras or centuries. The differences between the centuries were significantly varied and unique in the context of human deportment, customs, traditions, attitudes, and expectations, as acknowledged by many historians.[37] The pursuit of etiquette has been a societal concern for thousands of years. Martin Luther published a book of table manners in the sixteenth century. There were at least sixty new etiquette books published in nineteenth-century England.[38] Manners and deportment are timely, as well as regional affairs, which are alterable and were constantly transformed along with the changing society. These social behaviors and demeanors should not be regarded merely as details of little consequence, for they are an expression of an era as much as the changes in dress or any other outward manifestation of a particular period.

Theoretically, clothing fashion is a culturally endorsed style of aesthetic expression in dress and adornment, which is discernible at any given time and changes over time within a social system of a group of associated individuals.[39]

---

[35] Marybelle Bigelow, *Fashion in History: Western Dress, Prehistoric to Present* (London: Pearson College Div, 1979), 3.

Diana Crane, *Fashion and its Social Agendas: Class, Gender, and Identity in Clothing.* (Chicago: The University of Chicago Press, 1933).

[36] - in any historical study literary texts should be interpreted within the appropriate historical and theoretical context -

[37] Joan Wildeblood, *The Polite World: A Guide to English Manners and Deportment* (London: Davis Poynter Ltd, 1965).

[38] Joseph Dent, Australian Etiquette: Rules and Usage of the Best Society (London: D. E. McConnell, 1980).

Marion Fletcher, *Costume in Australia* (Melbourne: Oxford UP, 1984).

Margaret Maynard, *Fashioned from Penury: Dress as Cultural Practice in Colonial Australia* (Cambridge: The Press Syndicate of the University of Cambridge, 1994).

[39] George B. Sproles, "Fashion Theory: a Conceptual Framework," in *Advances in Consumer Research*, Volume 01, eds. Scott Ward and Peter Wright, Ann Abor, (Association for Consumer Research, 1974), 463-472.

George B. Sproles & Leslie Burns. *Changing Appearances, Understanding Dress in Contemporary Society* (New York: Fairchild Publications, 1989).

As argued by many writers,[40] similar to the differences in etiquette between the centuries, the differences in clothing styles were significant. The above phenomenon was not only restricted to upper-class clothing, but was also applied to some sections of the lower-classes. As Cunnington explains, the classification of household servants, their titles, occupation, and livery, was different and unique to each century, from the period between the Medieval and pre-twentieth centuries.[41] As do all other works of art, clothes reflect the times in which they were created. People reveal themselves unconsciously both in the art forms they accept, and those they reject.[42] The cutting and construction techniques also varied considerably from century to century as each era of the history of attire produced its own unique characteristics and silhouettes. In analyzing the above statement, the changes in clothing features within each one hundred years (especially between 1400-1900), was noteworthy. Especially from 1400 onwards, each century's attire had its own unique characteristics in style, fashion, and cutting and construction techniques, which were recognizable and unique to that particular century. To support that argument, Kroeber's fashion mutation theory suggested the fundamental feature changes in fashion developed on an average cycle of approximately one century.[43]

In concurrence with the main rationale of this study,[44] costumes throughout the ages have symbolically expressed the inner philosophical thoughts that directed the behavior of a given epoch.[45] Clothes exemplify the society and culture of a particular era and environment. The differences between clothing styles and fashion varied throughout pre-nineteenth centuries; therefore, the

---

[40] François Boucher, *A History of Costume in the West* (London: Thames and Hudson, 1966).
Norah Waugh, *The Cut of Women's Clothes 1600-1930* (London: Faber and Faber, 1968).
Geoffrey Squire, *Dress Art and Society 1560-1970* (London: Studio Vista, 1974).

[41] Phillis Cunnington, *Costume of Household Servants from the Middle Ages to 1900* (London: Adam and Charles Black, 1974).

[42] Rudolph Broby-Johansen, *Body and Clothes* (London: Faber and Faber Limited, 1968), 5.

[43] Gordon Wills & David Midgley, *Fashion Marketing: An Anthology of View Points and Perspectives* (London: Allen and Unwin Ltd, 1973), 12.

[44] –in any historical study literary texts should be interpreted within the appropriate historical and theoretical context–

[45] Marybelle Bigelow, *Fashion in History: Western Dress, Prehistoric to Present* (London: Pearson College Div, 1979), 3.
Anne Hollander, *Sex and Suits* (New York: Alfred A. Knoff, 1995). 4.

differences between clothing/fashion principles and reasonings also varied and were unique to each century. According to Francois Boucher,[46] the vocabulary of costume, its application, and its meaning, varied with the period. In the context of the natural height of humans throughout the centuries, Carl Kohler, in his *A History of Costume*, discusses the significant differences between the stature of people of the earlier centuries, arguing men and women in the twentieth century have apparently grown stouter and taller, compared with the pre-nineteenth centuries. Very few men or women today can don the ancient clothing. This is the case even with garments of the nineteenth century. Clothes of the Empire period and those of the Biedermeier style[47] are astonishingly small, and even more astonishing are the small measurements of the previous centuries, e.g., sixteenth-century clothes discovered in the Wittelsbach mausolcum at St Martin-in-Lauingen in Wiirtemberg.[48]

As Broby-Johansen examines, the history of dress is full of deception and self-delusion, deliberate and unconscious mistakes, the calculated and uncalculated in a long and illogical record of human folly. In short, it is simply the history of humankind. The interplay between the two genders, with the whole range of shifting emotions that it encompasses, forms a mirror in which the ever-changing world of fashion is reflected. Dress does not merely show how men and women wish to appear; it provides answers to many questions and also a criticism of the people who ask them. Women's fashions through the ages can provide a mass of silent evidence against the tyranny of the male at various times, and men's fashions can make out an equally strong case against the female gender. These situations occur because each gender reacts in accordance with the demands of the opposite. In a subtle way, the nature of one gender is revealed in the concealment of the other.[49]

Furthermore, a change of ideas, ideals, or conditions of life in any society is often responsible for a change in fashion/attire. In confirming with the primary

---

[46] François Boucher, *A History of Costume in the West* (London: Thames and Hudson, 1966), 5-6.

[47] **Biedermeier style**: In art, transitional period between Neoclassicism and Romanticism as it was interpreted by the bourgeoisie, particularly in Germany, Austria, northern Italy, and the Scandinavian countries. (Britannica, T. Editors of Encyclopaedia. "Biedermeier style." Encyclopedia Britannica, November 8, 2012. https://www.britannica.com/art/Biedermeier-style.)

[48] Carl Kohler, *A History of Costume* (New York: Dover Publications, 1963), 55.

[49] Rudolph Broby-Johansen, Body and Clothes (London: Faber and Faber Limited, 1968), 5.

objective,[50] in the East, where civilization has remained constant for many centuries, clothing and fashions have remained comparatively stable. Among the Western nations, on the other hand, where there has been a constant mingling of nationalities, fashions, and clothing have very frequently changed as a result of changed environmental, political, economic, sociological, and societal conditions. In regards to environmental conditions, for instance, among the earliest civilized peoples, whose home was along the shores of the Mediterranean, fashions took the form of loose, flowing garments. Men soon found, however, that an active life made clothing of this sort impossible, and, as a result, tight, well-fitted garments were adopted. Women, whose life activities made changes of this sort unnecessary, continued to wear loose, flowing garments without change or modification. In term of social ideals, especially those related to religion, are well reflected in the dress of the people. During the eleventh and twelfth centuries, European dress was dominated in form and color by the Catholic Church, and the secular costumes of men and women closely resembled those of the different ecclesiastical bodies. Even as late as the fifteenth century, Italian fashions continued to show this influence. Then, with the revival of interest in the learning of the past, and with the acceptance of Renaissance ideals, clothing so reflected this changed point of view that the dress for ladies set the pattern for dress for the saints.[51]

Whilst the analysis of fashion and attire has been attempted in many facets by historians, anthropologists, literary theorists, and social psychologists, such as Thorstein Veblen, Carl Flugel, Max Von Boehn, James Laver or Quentin Bell, towards the latter part of the twentieth century, challenging contemporary ideology and interpretations have emerged beyond the range of feminist concepts as well as populist or post-modern phenomena. As referred to by Hendrickson,[52] many of these novel analyses focus on marginalized social categories such as women, homosexual people, and ethnic minorities in the late twentieth century capitalist context. These recent assignments consider attire as both signs and commodities enmeshed in multiple webs of meaning

---

[50] –in any historical study literary texts should be interpreted within the appropriate historical and theoretical context–

[51] Elizabeth B. Hurlock, *The Psychology of Dress: An Analysis of Fashion and Its Motive*, (New York: B. Blom, 1971), 52-220.

[52] Hildi Hendrikson, *Clothing and Difference: Embodied Identities in Colonial and Post-modern Africa*, (London: Duke UP, 1996), 3-4.

and value. "Such studies may explore the repressive power of fashion as a commodity.'[53]

Another angle to the main rationale of this chapter,[54] conceivably, is that gender-based concepts such as the theories of eroticism, fetishism, and sexuality were significantly prominent in the context of explosive and expansive contemporary interpretations of costume. Perspectives and acceptances have alternated, rotated, terminated, replaced, restored, reversed, and substituted throughout the centuries. Lady Godiva, an eleventh-century noblewoman, has been honored through centuries for riding naked through the town of Coventry on a mission of philanthropy. Superstition and State policy burned Joan of Arc at the stake, but men now raise statues to her heroic memory.[55]

"Fetishism like pornography, seems to be a relatively modern invention."[56] Until the twentieth century, underwear such as stays corsets, panniers, crinolines, and bustles were regarded as popular fashion accessories. However, in the post-twentieth century societies, wearing tight fitted, laced, and sculptured clothing is more of a reflection of one's sexual, erotic, and voluptuous preferences. David Kunzel, who compiled an exclusive research on "Fashion and Fetishism: A Social History of the Corset, Tight Lacing and Other Forms of Body-Sculpture in the West" analyses fetishism as a motivated force which sexual instinct puts onto an aspect of dress.[57] In concurrence with the above assertion, Valerie Steel theorizes, "All my research has led to me to believe that, at the deepest level, the meaning of clothing in general and fashion in particular is erotic."[58] These gender-related issues reflect the significant relationship between culture and clothing in any given society.

Some determining factors of the main objective rely on questions such as: To what extent do the major cultural and social forms change through time? Or, to what extent have cultural systems changed or remained the same since?

---

[53] Shari Benstock and Suzanne Ferris, *On Fashion*, (New Jersey: Rutgers UP, 1994), 8.

[54] –in any historical study literary texts should be interpreted within the appropriate historical and theoretical context–

[55] *The Illustrated Manners Book: A Manual of Good Behavior and Polite Accomplishments*, New York: Leland, Clay, & Co., 1855), 143.

[56] Valerie Steel, *Fetish, Fashion, Sex and Power*, (London: Oxford UP, 1996), 21.

[57] David Kunzle. *Fashion and Fetishism: A Social History of the Corset, Tight Lacing and Other Forms of Body-Sculpture in the West*, (New Jersey: Rowman and Littlefield, 1982).

[58] Valerie Steel, *Fetish, Fashion, Sex and Power*, (London: Oxford UP, 1996), 5.

However, world-historical occurrences, such as the French Revolution, World Wars (political events), political movements such as Chartism, socialism, and feminism, as well as the subsequent changes in popular attitudes, social structure, and society (Industrial Revolution, mass production, modernization, and urbanization), have been uniquely attributed to the transformation and mutation of fashion and clothing, which is incomparably significant to the late nineteenth and twentieth centuries. Undoubtedly, these modern, innovative conceptual ideologies and interpretations potentially expanded the existing theories and philosophies or perhaps enhanced the discipline to a certain extent.

In coherence with the main objective of the chapter,[59] the last millennium has been shaped by successive waves of change, with the leading drivers, such as law and order in the Twelfth century, markets in the Thirteenth century, the scientific revolution in the Seventeenth century, the French Revolution in the Eighteenth century, communications revolution in the Nineteenth century and the inventions of the future in the twentieth century, etc. Also, each century, especially between 1400 and 1900, with brief transitional periods between, produced its unique style and fashion, which was symbolic of that particular era. Changes in vestimentary codes, decorative details, such as trimmings, draping, and accessories, represented the taste of society and the inclination of the period. Although the changes in patterns and cuts were gradual and evolved from the previous style, the centuries' distinctiveness was still perceivable in new materials. As every century and millennium is different in the societal, economic, technological, sociological, and ideological contexts, theoretically, they should be understood and defined in similar contexts.

In conclusion, the clothing of humanity is full of profound significance, for the human spirit not only builds its own body, but also fashions its own dress, even though, for the most part, it leaves the actual construction to other hands. Clothing and fashions for women show greater variability than fashions for men in contemporary civilization. Not only do women's fashions change more rapidly and completely, but the total gamut of allowed forms is greater for women than for men. In times past and in other cultures, however, men's fashions show a greater exuberance than women's.[60] The manner of study in

---

[59] –in any historical study literary texts should be interpreted within the appropriate historical and theoretical context–

[60] Edward Sapir, "Fashion" in *Encyclopedia of the Social Sciences VI* (New York: Macmillan, 1931), 139-141.

ancient times differed from that of the modern age in that the former was the proper and complete formation of the natural consciousness.[61] Men and women dress themselves in accordance with the dictates of that great unknown, the Spirit of the Time,[62] or Zeitgeist; as Georg Wilhelm Friedrich Hegel believed, everything in the world was in constant motion: every individual life, nature, history, society. This results in each epoch having its own particular zeitgeist, or general spirit. One historical epoch is not randomly followed by another; instead, there is a principle of logical evolution, the general trend of thought, feeling, or tastes characteristic of a particular period, therefore, must be understood and interpreted accordingly.[63]

"There is a fickle, teasing Goddess,
Fantastic in her tastes, playful in adornment,
Who at every season seems to flee, return and
Rise again.
Proteus was her father, her name is Fashion."
- Voltaire[64]

Bibliography

Barnard, Malcolm. "Fashion Theory: A Reader," in *Costume and Fashion.* London, New York: 2007.

Bell, Quentin. *On Human Finery.* London: The Hogarth Press, 1976.

Benstock. Shari and Ferris, Suzanne . *On Fashion.* New Jersey: Rutgers UP, 1994.

Bigelow, Marybelle. *Fashion in History: Western Dress, Prehistoric to Present.* London: Pearson College Div, 1979.

Blumer, Herbert. 1968 "Fashion." in *International Encyclopedia of the Social Sciences* V. New York: Macmillan, 1968.

Boucher, François. *A History of Costume in the West.* London: Thames and Hudson, 1966.

Broby-Johansen, Rudolf. *Body and Clothes.* London: Faber and Faber Limited, 1968.

---

[61] Georg Wilhelm Friedrich Hegel, The Phenomenology of Spirit (Delhi: motilal Banarsidass Publishers Private Limited, 1998), 19

[62] Carl Kohler, *A History of Costume* (New York: Dover Publications, 1963), 57.

[63] https://www.dw.com/en/hegel-the-philosopher-who-viewed-history-as-inevitable-progress/a-54707032.

[64] Elizabeth B. Hurlock, *The Psychology of Dress: An Analysis of Fashion and Its Motive.* New York: B. Blom, 1971, 3.

Brooks Young, Agnes. *Recurring Cycles of Fashion: 1760-1937.* New York: Harper & Brothers, 1937).

Cannington, Phillis. *Costume of Household Servants from the Middle Ages to 1900.* London: Adam and Charles Black, 1974.

Carlyle, Thomas. *Sartor Resartus,* London: Dent, 1984.

Chaucer, Geoffrey. *Canterbury Tales.* New York: Garden City Publishing Company, 1934.

Crane, Diana. *Fashion and its Social Agendas: Class, Gender, and Identity in Clothing.* Chicago: The University of Chicago Press, 1933.

Cunnington, Phillis. *Costume of Household Servants from the Middle Ages to 1900,* London: Adam and Charles Black, 1974.

Dent, Joseph. *Australian Etiquette: Rules and Usage of the Best Society.* London: D. E. McConnell, 1980.

Durant, Will. *The Story of Philosophy.* London: Ernest Benn, 1927.

Eluwawalage, Damayanthie. "Dress Theory: Exploring Critical Issues" in *Trending Now,* eds. Laura Petican, Mariam Esseghaier, Angela Nurse, Damayanthie Eluwawalage. London: Inter-disciplinary Press, 2013 ISBN: 978-1-84888-211-9, File type: eBook, 103-113.

Fleming, Grace. "The Importance of Historic Context in Analysis and Interpretation." *ThoughtCo.* https://www.thoughtco.com/what-is-historical-context-1857069 (accessed February 23, 2023).

Fletcher, Marion. *Costume in Australia.* Melbourne: Oxford UP, 1984.

Flower, Cedric. *Clothes in Australia: A Pictorial History 1788-1980.* Sydney: Kangaroo Press, 1984.

Hendrikson, Hildi. *Clothing and Difference: Embodied Identities in Colonial and Post-modern Africa.* London: Duke UP, 1996.

Hollander, Anne. *Sex and Suits.* New York: Alfred A. Knoff, 1995.

Hurlock, Elizabeth. *The Psychology of Dress: An Analysis of Fashion and Its Motive.* New York: B. Blom, 1971.

Kohler, Carl. *A History of Costume.* New York: Dover Publications, 1963.

Kunzel, David. *Fashion and Fetishism: A Social History of the Corset, Tight Lacing and Other Forms of Body-Sculpture in the West,* New Jersey: Rowman and Littlefield, 1982.

Laver, James. *Taste and Fashion.* London: George G. Harrap and Company Ltd, 1937.

Lurie, Alison. *The Language of Clothes.* London: William Heinemann Ltd, 1981.

Maynard, Margaret. *Fashioned from Penury: Dress as Cultural Practice in Colonial Australia.* Cambridge: The Press Syndicate of the University of Cambridge, 1994.

Richardson, Jane. and Kroeber, Alfred. *Anthropological Records* 5: 111-153, Collective Dynamics. "Three centuries of women's dress fashions: a quantitative analysis." New York: Crowell, 1947.

Sapir, Edward. "Fashion" in *Encyclopedia of the Social Sciences VI.* New York: Macmillan, 1931.

Simmel, Georg. *Essays on Sociology, Philosophy and Aesthetics.* New York: Harper Torch Books, 1959.

Simmel, Georg. "Fashion" in *American Journal of Sociology* 62:541-558. (reprint), 1957.

Sproles, George. 1974 "Fashion Theory: A Conceptual Framework" in *NA - Advances in Consumer Research* Volume 01, eds. Scott Ward and Peter Wright, Ann Abor, MI: Association for Consumer Research. 463-472.

Sproles, George. & Burns, Leslie. *Changing Appearances, Understanding Dress in Contemporary Society.* New York: Fairchild Publications, 1989.

Squire, Geoffrey. *Dress, Art and Society 1560-1970.* London: Studio Vista, 1974.

Steel, Valerie. *Fetish, Fashion, Sex and Power.* London: Oxford UP, 1996.

Veblen, Thorstein. *The Theory of the Leisure Class.* London: Unwin Books, 1899.

Waugh, Norah. *The Cut of Women's Clothes 1600-1930.* London: Faber and Faber, 1968.

Wildblood, Joan. *The Polite World: A Guide to English Manners and Deportment.* London: Davis Poynter Ltd, 1965.

Wilhelm Friedrich Hegel, Georg. *The Phenomenology of Spirit.* Delhi: Motilal Banarsidass Publishers Private Limited, 1998.

Looking Ahead while Reflecting Back

A Volume Conclusion

This volume is an invitation to researchers, students, enthusiasts, and the general public to take the topic of clothing, costume, and fashion seriously. Also, In the realms of attire, primarily because of its very widespread influence in public and private spheres in every society, it would be impossible to consider or analyze it from every angle within the limits of one publication.

From a historical perspective on understanding dress, it is decisively important to look back and analyze how fashion and related studies have moved on and how twenty-first century thought, practice, habitude, and mode differ from the past, especially in this era of cultural and societal disparity and divergence. The volume aims to show a number of incidences of this meaningfulness by presenting diverse investigations of dress from the past in which its cultural and practical usefulness, its persuasiveness and expressiveness, are undeniable. Yet additional research is necessary as clothing lessons from the past might inspire more current cohesiveness.

Chapter One, "Pattern to Pate: An Examination of Early Modern Embroidered English Head-Coverings and their Sources" is an area of historic clothing that would benefit from further exploration, including topics such as the importance of hair taping and understructure and the lack of visual evidence of the coif and cap by the monarchs Elizabeth I and James I and VI.

The impact of a woman's hair taping on the sixteenth and seventeenth century coif is fundamental. The coif has a very unique shape that only works with an understructure. This is in marked contrast to the equivalent man's head covering, the cap, which sits lightly on top of the head without regard to the hair (or lack thereof). Integrating this structural element into the understanding, display, and discussion of women's coifs is necessary for the ongoing research.

There were scarcely any portraits or paintings of Queen Elizabeth I and King James I and VI wearing an embroidered coif or cap, even though they were not uncommon among the elites of their court and country. Unlike Charles Howard, who did commission a portrait of himself in his regalia and an embroidered cap, James is never portrayed wearing one himself, even when depicted in regalia similar to Howard's. Indeed, the Trevelyon Miscellany 1608 and 1616 manuscripts both contain over twenty men's cap patterns with elaborate embroidery designs, which indicates that these were still in fashion during James's reign, possibly due to his more severe Scottish fashion traditions. Though his clothing might look elaborate to our modern eyes, his clothes are relatively plain in comparison with those of his contemporaries at the English court. Could his eschewing of embroidered coifs have been a personal choice? In-depth research into any extant inventories, warrants, or letters from his court could be an important area of exploration for future researchers.

Comprehensively, the relatively narrow scope of the limited production and use of embroidered caps and coifs, made and used only by the elite and only in their homes, would seem to be a small, niche area of fashion research. However, as the chapter discussed, even this circumscribed corner of clothing and textile history can provide a wide range of further inquiry.

It seems that enough has been said about the evolution of fight costumes in the major fight promotions of the world. However, according to **Chapter Two**, "In It to Win It: The Evolution of Fightwear in Mixed Martial Arts Combat Sports," the topic of fight costumes in the world of MMA is not completely exhausted. Further studies can be done on the now defunct PRIDE Fighting Championship and the pre-fight introduction costumes fighters used. PRIDE was quite unique in that the fighter introductions included an entire performance wherein fighters had customized thematic costumes that were combined with their introductory music. Additionally, the fighters made their way to the fighter inspection area with performers, and some fighters even choreographed dance routines with their performers. Upon reaching the pre-fight fighter inspection area, fighters would then take off their pre-fight costumes, revealing their fightwear before entering the combat area. The more recent promotion, ONE Championship, also allows its fighters to walk to the pre-fight inspection area in a somewhat similar manner. Some fighters, such as the two-time champion Stamp Fairtax, will occasionally wear a customized pre-fight costume and dance on her way to the fight inspection area. She nor any of the other fighters have accompanying performers. However, a study of the customized and thematic pre-fight costumes and how they may be relevant to the fighter's life or the narrative they are portraying prior to the fight is a very interesting analysis to pursue. Although a study of this sort expands our knowledge and understanding of the evolution of fight costumes and their usage within the world of MMA, this particular aspect of the topic was not covered in this present analysis as it was beyond the scope of the study.

Another area of particular interest that may be taken up in the future is how the fight costumes used by different martial artists affected their fight strategy. It has been noted throughout this present work that nearly all fighters chose their fight attire as they were trying to achieve victory over their opponent in the most efficient way possible. Therefore, it is obvious that fighters chose their fight costumes with a particular strategy in mind for the upcoming martial combat. As a result of the fight costume chosen, different strategies were employed by each fighter to achieve lesser or greater success. Depending on the outcome of the fight, fighters could and would make changes to their fight costumes in the pursuit of victory. Therefore, a study of how combatants used their fight costumes to achieve their aims and what strategies were employed depending on the fight costume is not only interesting but furthers the dialogue on this particular topic. As with the pre-fight costumes, though, this particular subtopic of fight strategy combined with fight costumes could not be covered in great depth in the present study as it is, unfortunately, beyond the scope of the present work.

Chapter Three, "Attire and Narrative in Virgil's *Aeneid*," investigates the narrative use of clothing, or written dress. Besides its importance as adornment indicative of cultural and historical details, it also serves as a literary tool that shapes, structures, and advances the plot. This represents an underdeveloped area of study of the narrative use of clothing by the ancient bards and their use of dress to transfer social, cultural, and political messages. One might well ask what the Ancient World has to tell our contemporary one. Yet the oft heard saying that history repeats itself holds true. Stories about the rise and fall of empires structured through what people wore can suggest cultural and political parallels between these worlds. Because articles of clothing cannot be taken to task or held responsible for errors, they communicate with any reader who has a cultural/political understanding of the era in which the text is written. Here, we have connections between dress and politics in Ancient Rome, yet our global world needs stories from all parts, and many, like Virgil's *Aeneid* contain a sartorial structure of meaningfulness. Although some have been accomplished, more explorations into written dress are required from places like India, China, Africa, and others. These investigations can expand cultural and political understanding, offering further clarity that must propel unity. More parallels drawn between our world and the past contribute to a more cohesive, extensive, and instructive field of study.

Chapter Four, "Historical Costume: Acknowledging the Distinctiveness Between the Centuries and Epochs," only looks at sixteenth- to twentieth-century clothing, fashion, and dress-related theories. The study points to three directions for future research. First, further research should reach beyond the twentieth century towards the twenty-first century; secondly, there is a need for further inquiry into the theories that can be applicable to colonial contexts, and thirdly, the study should be expanded to explore children's clothing, aboriginal/tribal clothing, ethnic clothing, occupational clothing, leisure clothing, and charity clothing.

In collating with the above, as George Sproles[1] explains, the generalized theoretical concept of fashion in the twentieth century varied in the context of definitional perspectives of the pre-twentieth centuries. For instance, in the psychological point of view, the twentieth century definition of fashion is "a series of recurring changes in the choices of a group of people, which, though they may be accompanied by utility, are not determined by it"[2]; in the economical and marketing perspective, "Fashion is nothing more or less than the prevailing style at any given time"[3]; according to retailer Alfred Daniels, "Fashion is a conception of what is currently appropriate"[4]; sociologists Lang and Lang treat fashion as "an elementary form of collective behavior, whose compelling power lies in the implicit judgment of an anonymous multitude"[5]; economist Robinson offers fashion definitions: "Fashion, defined in its most general sense, is the pursuit of novelty for its own sake"[6]; Fashion is "change in the design of things for decorative purposes"[7]; in the marketing context,

---

[1] George Sproles, "*Fashion Theory: a Conceptual Framework,*" in *Advances in Consumer Research* Volume 01, eds. Scott Ward and Peter Wright, Ann Abor, MI: Association for Consumer Research (1974), 463-472.

[2] Elizabeth Hurlock, *The Psychology of Dress: An Analysis of Fashion and Its Motive,* (New York: B. Blom, 1971).

[3] Paul Nystrom, *Economics of fashion* (New York: Ronald Press, 1928).

[4] Christopher M. Miller, Shelby H. McIntyre and Murali K. Mantrala, *Toward Formalizing Fashion Theory,*
Journal of Marketing Research, Vol. 30, No. 2 (May, 1993), 142-157.

[5] Jane Richardson, and Alfred Kroeber, Anthropological Records 5: 111-153, Collective Dynamics. "*Three centuries of women's dress fashions: a quantitative analysis.*" (New York: Crowell, 1947).

[6] Dwight Robinson, *Fashion Theory and Product Design.* Harvard Business Review, (1958), 36, 126-138.

[7] Dwight Robinson, *The Economics of Fashion Demand.* Quarterly Journal of Economics, (1961), 75, 376-398.

"Fashion adoption is a process of social contagion by which a new style or product is adopted by the consumer after commercial introduction by the designer or manufacturer"[8]; home economist Horn defines fashion as "a manifestation of collective behavior, and as such represents the popular, accepted, prevailing style at any given time"[9]; and Webster's Unabridged Dictionary offers fashion as "the make or form of anything; style, shape, appearance, or mode of structure; also, peculiar shape or style."

Attire and fashion have been traditionally viewed as a clothing-specific phenomenon. Therefore, the development of a novel and contemporary fashion theory may be conceptually structured for application to a wide range of twenty-first century phenomena, as it can be correlated with a far-reaching gamut of social, psychological, economic, and gender-related concepts, constructs, and principles.

Dress is a universal concept, and everyone in every culture clothes themselves in some way, both in their private and public life. It is a complex combination where each version of dress becomes a rich cultural text that disperses information and is thus useful in drawing parallels between past and present civilizations. In this context, looking back helps us see that many things do not change. There are sartorial lessons to be learned, and this recognition impels the hope of stimulating more scholarship in areas where the literature and research are not yet fully developed, and the future volumes and related research will extend this effort. Also, far-reaching scholarship could be added and momentously enhanced by the above-mentioned further studies and the inclusion of how fashion/clothing-related studies have moved on and how twenty-first century thought differs from past theorists and past centuries, because it is central to the theme of the interplay of historical perspective on understanding dress, which this publication so pertinently addresses.

Bibliography

Horn, Marilyn. *The Second Skin.* Boston: Houghton Mifflin, 1968.

Hurlock, Elizabeth. *The Psychology of Dress: An Analysis of Fashion and Its Motive.* New York: B. Blom, 1971.

King, Charles. *The Innovator in the Fashion Adoption Process,* in Reflections on progress in marketing. Chicago: American Marketing Association, 1964.

---

[8] Charles King, *The Innovator in the Fashion Adoption Process,* in *Reflections on progress in marketing.* (Chicago: American Marketing Association, 1964).

[9] Marilyn Horn, *The Second Skin* (Boston: Houghton Mifflin, 1968).

Miller, Christopher, McIntyre Shelby and Mantrala, Murali. *Toward Formalizing Fashion Theory*, Journal of Marketing Research, Vol. 30, No. 2 (May, 1993).

Nystrom, Paul. *Economics of fashion*. New York: Ronald Press, 1928.

Richardson, Jane. and Kroeber, Alfred. *Anthropological Records* 5: 111-153, Collective Dynamics. "Three centuries of women's dress fashions: a quantitative analysis." New York: Crowell, 1947.

Robinson, Dwight. *Fashion Theory and Product Design*. Harvard Business Review, (1958).

Robinson, Dwight. *The Economics of Fashion Demand*. Quarterly Journal of Economics, (1961).

Sproles, George. "*Fashion Theory: a Conceptual Framework,*" in *Advances in Consumer Research* Volume 01, eds. Scott Ward and Peter Wright, Ann Abor, MI: Association for Consumer Research (1974).

List of Contributors

Damayanthie Eluwawalage, PhD, MPHA - Professional Historian, Assistant Professor, Private Pilot, Aerospace Education Officer (Civil Air Patrol, United States Air Force Auxiliary), NASA Research Scientist, and Industrial, Product and Fashion Designer. She earned her doctorate in design/history from Edith Cowan University, Australia. She also holds a BA (Honours First-class) in Design from Curtin University of Technology, Australia. She is an Assistant Professor at Delaware State University and a Professional Historian who specializes in costume history. Her multidisciplinary research interests include interdisciplinary design, industrial/product design, design theory, aviation/space history, space/aviation (she holds a Private Pilot License), costume history, fashion/aesthetic theory, space suit design concepts/applications, lunar dust mitigation technologies, oxygen/gas mask design/technologies, and general aviation.

Linda Matheson, PhD, holds an interdisciplinary doctorate from the University of California at Davis, where until 2022 she lectured in the Department of Comparative Literature. She also taught in the Departments of Textiles and Clothing, Gender Studies and Women's Studies. Her dissertation, *Divinely Attired*, examines the contribution of dress to the narrative process of Ancient Epics and Sacred Texts such as *The Epic of Gilgamesh*, the book of "Genesis," the *Rāmāyaṇa*, the *Mahābhārata*, and the *Aeneid*. Using modern western social theory, it explores the interweaving of written dress, and image as vehicle of character and cultural development. She publishes both nationally and internationally and is currently working on the *Rhetoric of the Images from the Cantigas of Santa Maria* (12th century Spain).

Jeremiah Snyder completed his Master's in History at the University of Colorado in Colorado Springs in 2014. Having studied Greek and Roman history by reading primary source material while also focusing his efforts on the history of the United States from its entry in World War I onward, Jeremiah has an extensive background in the Humanities with interests that concentrate on the intersections of Western arts, religion and politics. After some years of teaching humanities courses at the collegiate level, Jeremiah now works conducting research for a law firm in the Denver, Colorado, area. In his free time, he loves to be outdoors in the beautiful Rocky Mountains with his wife, two children, and other family members, and writing when he can.

Christy Gordon Baty is an Eleanor M. Garvey Fellow in Printing and Graphic Arts at the Houghton Rare Books Library at Harvard University. Christy graduated with a Master's in History from the University of Nebraska at Kearney; her thesis focused on the needlework of English women in the early modern era. She earned her undergraduate degree in English Literature from the University of California, Berkeley. Christy is a member of the American Historical Association, Honor Society of Phi Kappa Phi, Phi Alpha Theta, and the Embroiderers' Guild of America.

Erin Harvey Moody is a certified Collections Manager of Costume and Textiles. She has taught aspects of historical fashion for many years and is a member of the Costume Society, UK. Erin studied historical embroidery technique at The Royal School of Needlework, and holds a PgCert in Museum Education from the University of Glasgow. Erin's primary work has been the cultural influence of needlework and fashion in early modern England. She is a member of the Royal Historical Society, and an Eleanor M. Garvey Fellow in Printing and Graphic Arts at the Houghton Rare Books Library at Harvard University.

Index

A

B

C

D

E

F

G

P

Q

R

S

www.ingramcontent.com/pod-product-compliance
Lightning Source LLC
LaVergne TN
LVHW020633100826
845148LV00012B/2163

* 9 7 9 8 8 8 1 9 0 1 9 0 5 *